# Can We Avoid Another
# Financial Crisis?

'et

The Future of Capitalism series

Steve Keen

––––––––––

# Can We Avoid Another Financial Crisis?

polity

First published in 2017 by Polity Press
Reprinted 2017 (five times)

Polity Press
65 Bridge Street
Cambridge CB2 1UR, UK

Polity Press
350 Main Street
Malden, MA 02148, USA

ISBN-13: 978-1-5095-1372-7
ISBN-13: 978-1-5095-1373-4(pb)

A catalogue record for this book is available from the British Library.

Library of Congress Cataloging-in-Publication Data

Names: Keen, Steve, author.
Title: Can we avoid another financial crisis? / Steve Keen.
Description: Malden, MA : Polity, 2017. | Series: The future of capitalism |
    Includes bibliographical references and index.
Identifiers: LCCN 2016044967| ISBN 9781509513727 (hardback) | ISBN
    9781509513734 (paperback)
Subjects: LCSH: Economic policy. | Political planning. | Debt. | Financial
    crises. | BISAC: POLITICAL SCIENCE / Public Policy / Economic Policy.
Classification: LCC HD87 .K434 2017 | DDC 338.5/42--dc23
LC record available at https://lccn.loc.gov/2016044967

Typeset in 11 on 15 Sabon by
Servis Filmsetting Ltd, Stockport, Cheshire
Printed and bound in the UK by CPI Group (UK) Ltd, Croydon, CR0 4YY

For further information on Polity, visit our website:
politybooks.com

# Contents

# Acknowledgements

My biggest intellectual debts are to the deceased non-mainstream economists Hyman Minsky, Richard Goodwin, Wynne Godley and John Blatt. I have also benefited from interactions with many academic colleagues – most notably Trond Andresen, Bob Ayres, Dirk Bezemer, Gael Giraud, David Graeber, Matheus Grasselli, Michael Hudson, Michael Kumhof, Marc Lavoie, Russell Standish and Devrim Yilmaz – and the philanthropist Richard Vague. Funding from the Institute for New Economic Thinking and from the public via Kickstarter has also been essential to my work.

This book could not have been written but for the work of the Bank of International Settlements in assembling comprehensive databases on private and government debt and house prices for the world economy.[1] This continues a tradition of which

# Acknowledgements

the BIS can be proud: it was the only formal economic body to provide any warning of the Global Financial Crisis of 2008 before it happened,[2] thanks to the appreciation that its then Research Director Bill White had of Hyman Minsky's 'Financial Instability Hypothesis' (Minsky, 1972, 1977), at a time when it was more fashionable in economics to ignore Minsky than to cite him.

# List of Tables and Figures

All figures and tables were produced by the author using publicly available data, unless otherwise stated.

# List of Tables and Figures

# List of Tables and Figures

# 1

# From Triumph to Crisis in Economics

There was a time when the question this book poses would have generated derisory guffaws from leading economists – and that time was not all that long ago. In December 2003, the Nobel Prize winner Robert Lucas began his Presidential Address to the *American Economic Association* with the triumphant claim that economic crises like the Great Depression were now impossible:

> Macroeconomics was born as a distinct field in the 1940s, as a part of the intellectual response to the Great Depression. The term then referred to the body of knowledge and expertise that we hoped would prevent the recurrence of that economic disaster. My thesis in this lecture is that macroeconomics in this original sense has succeeded: *Its central problem of depression prevention has been solved, for all practical purposes, and has in fact*

1

*been solved for many decades.* (Lucas, 2003, p. 1, emphasis added)

Four years later, that claim fell apart, as first the USA and then the global economy entered the deepest and longest crisis since the Great Depression. Almost a decade later, the recovery from that crisis is fragile at best. The question of whether another financial crisis may occur can no longer be glibly dismissed.

That question was first posed decades earlier by the then unknown but now famous maverick American economist Hyman Minsky. Writing two decades before Lucas, Minsky remarked that 'The most significant economic event of the era since World War II is something that has not happened: there has not been a deep and long-lasting depression' (1982, p. ix).[1] In contrast, before the Second World War, 'serious recessions happened regularly . . . to go more than thirty-five years without a severe and protracted depression is a striking success'. To Minsky, this meant that the most important questions in economics were:

Can 'It' – a Great Depression – happen again? And if 'It' can happen, why didn't 'It' occur in the years since World War II? These are questions that naturally follow from both the historical record and the comparative success of the past thirty-five years. (1982, p. xii)

Minsky's ultimate conclusion was that crises in pure free-market capitalism were inevitable, because thanks to its financial system, capitalism 'is inherently flawed, being prone to booms, crises, and depressions:

> This instability, in my view, is due to characteristics the financial system must possess if it is to be consistent with full-blown capitalism. Such a financial system will be capable of both generating signals that induce an accelerating desire to invest and of financing that accelerating investment. (Minsky, 1969, p. 224)

A serious crisis hadn't occurred since the Second World War, Minsky argued, because the post-war economy was not a pure free-market system, but rather was a mixed market–state economy where the state was five times larger than it was before the Great Depression. A crisis had been prevented because spending by 'Big Government' during recessions had prevented 'the collapse of profits which is a necessary condition for a deep and long depression' (Minsky, 1982, p. xiii).

Given that Minsky reached this conclusion in

1982, and that Lucas's claim that the problem 'of depression prevention has been solved . . . for many decades' occurred in 2003, you might think that Lucas, like Minsky, thought that 'Big Government' prevented depressions, and that this belief was proven false by the 2008 crisis.

If only it were that simple. In fact, Lucas had reached precisely the opposite opinions about the stability of capitalism and the desirable policy to Minsky, because the question that preoccupied him was not Minsky's 'Can "It" – a Great Depression – happen again?', but the rather more esoteric question 'Can we derive macroeconomic theory from microeconomics?'

Ever since Keynes wrote *The General Theory of Employment, Interest and Money* (1936), economists have divided their discipline into two components: 'microeconomics', which considers the behaviour of consumers and firms; and 'macroeconomics', which considers the behaviour of the economy as a whole. Microeconomics has always been based on a model of consumers who aimed to maximise their utility, firms that aimed to maximise their profits, and a market system that achieved equilibrium between these two forces by equating supply and demand in every market. Macroeconomics before Lucas, on the other hand, was based on a mathematical interpretation of Keynes's attempt to explain why the Great Depression occurred, which was developed not by Keynes but by his contemporary John Hicks.

Though Hicks himself regarded his IS-LM model ('Investment-Savings & Liquidity-Money') as compatible with microeconomic theory (Hicks, 1981, p. 153; 1937, pp. 141–2), Lucas did not, because the model implied that government spending could boost aggregate demand during recessions. This was inconsistent with standard microeconomics, which argued that markets work best in the absence of government interventions.

Starting in the late 1960s, Lucas and his colleagues developed an approach to macroeconomics which was derived directly from standard microeconomic theory, which they called 'New Classical Macroeconomics'. In contrast to the IS-LM model, it asserted that, if consumers and firms were rational – which Lucas and his disciples interpreted to mean *(a) that consumers and firms modelled the future impact of government policies using the economic theory that Lucas and his colleagues had developed, and (b) that this theory accurately predicted the consequences of those policies* – then the government would be unable to alter aggregate demand because, whatever it did, the public would do the opposite:

> there is no sense in which the authority has the option to conduct countercyclical policy ... by virtue of the assumption that expectations are rational, there is no feedback rule that the authority can employ and expect to be able systematically to fool the public. (Sargent & Wallace, 1976, pp. 177–8)

Over the next few decades, this vision of a micro-founded macroeconomics in which the government was largely impotent led to the development of complicated mathematical models of the economy, which became known as 'Dynamic Stochastic General Equilibrium' (DSGE) models.

This intellectual process was neither peaceful nor apolitical. The first models, known as 'Real Business Cycle' (RBC) models, assumed that all markets worked perfectly, and asserted that all unemployment was voluntary – including the 25 per cent unemployment rates of the Great Depression (Prescott, 1999; Cole & Ohanian, 2004). This was too much for many economists, and what is now known as the 'Freshwater–Saltwater' divide developed within the mainstream of the profession.

The more politically progressive 'Saltwater' economists (who described themselves as 'New Keynesians') took the RBC models developed by their 'Freshwater' rivals and added in 'market imperfections' – which were also derived from standard microeconomic theory – to generate DSGE models. The market imperfections built into these models meant that if the model economy were disturbed from equilibrium by a 'shock', 'frictions' due to those imperfections would slow down the return to equilibrium, resulting in both slower growth and involuntary unemployment.

These 'New Keynesian' DSGE models came to dominate macroeconomic theory and policy around the world, and by 2007 they were the workhorse models of Treasuries and Central Banks. A representative (and, at the time, very highly regarded) DSGE model of the US economy had two types of firms (final goods producers operating in a 'perfect' market, and intermediate goods producers operating in an 'imperfect' one); one type of household (a worker–capitalist–bond trader amalgam that supplied labour via a trade union, earnt dividends from the two types of firms, and received interest income from government bonds); a trade union setting wages; and a government sector consisting of a revenue-constrained, bond-issuing fiscal authority and an activist Central Bank, which varied the interest rate in response to deviations of inflation and GDP growth from its target (Smets & Wouters, 2007).

Notably, a government that could affect

employment by fiscal policy was normally absent from DSGE models, as was a financial sector – and indeed money itself. The mindset that developed within the economics profession – and especially within Central Banks – was that these factors could be ignored in macroeconomics. Instead, if the Central Bank used DSGE models to guide policy, and therefore set the interest rate properly, economic growth and inflation would both reach desirable levels, and the economy would reach a Nirvana state of full employment and low inflation.

Right up until mid-2007, this model of the economy seemed to accurately describe the real world. Unemployment, which had peaked at 11 per cent in the USA in the 1983 recession, peaked at under 8 per cent in the early 1990s recession and just over 6 per cent in the early 2000s recession: the clear trend was for lower unemployment over time. Inflation, which had peaked at almost 15 per cent in 1980, peaked at just over 6 per cent in 1991 and under 4 per cent in the early 2000s: it was also heading down. New Keynesian economists believed that these developments showed that their management of the economy was working, and this vindicated their approach to economic modelling. They coined the term 'The Great Moderation' (Stock & Watson, 2002) to describe this period of falling peaks in unemployment and inflation, and attributed its occurrence to their management of the economy. Ex-Federal Reserve Chairman Ben Bernanke was particularly vocal in congratulating economists for this phenomenon:

> Recessions have become less frequent and milder, and quarter-to-quarter volatility in output and employment has declined significantly as well. The sources of the Great Moderation remain somewhat controversial, but as I have argued elsewhere, *there is evidence for the view that improved control of inflation has contributed in important measure to this welcome change in the economy.* (Bernanke, 2004, emphasis added)

Using DSGE models, official economics bodies like the OECD forecast that 2008 was going to be a bumper year. As 2007 commenced, unemployment in the USA was at the boom level of 4.5 per cent, inflation was right on the Federal Reserve's 2 per cent target, and according to the OECD in June of 2007, the future – for both the USA and the global economy – was bright:

> In its Economic Outlook last Autumn, the OECD took the view that the US slowdown was not heralding a period of worldwide economic weakness, unlike, for instance, in 2001. Rather, a 'smooth'

rebalancing was to be expected, with Europe taking over the baton from the United States in driving OECD growth.

Recent developments have broadly confirmed this prognosis. Indeed, *the current economic situation is in many ways better than what we have experienced in years*. Against that background, we have stuck to the rebalancing scenario. *Our central forecast remains indeed quite benign*: a soft landing in the United States, a strong and sustained recovery in Europe, a solid trajectory in Japan and buoyant activity in China and India. In line with recent trends, sustained growth in OECD economies would be underpinned by strong job creation and falling unemployment. (Cotis, 2007, emphasis added)

This rosy forecast was wrong even before it was published. US unemployment bottomed at 4.4 per cent in March 2007, and by December 2007 it had hit 5 per cent. By this stage, financial markets were in turmoil, but guided by their DSGE models, mainstream economists thought the increase in unemployment was not a major concern. In December 2007, David Stockton, Director of the Division of Research and Statistics at the Federal Reserve, assured its interest-rate-setting authority the Federal Open

Market Committee (FOMC) that there would be no recession in 2008:

> Overall, our forecast could admittedly be read as still painting a pretty benign picture: despite all the financial turmoil, the economy avoids recession and, even with steeply higher prices for food and energy and a lower exchange value of the dollar, we achieve some modest edging-off of inflation. (FOMC, 2007)

In stark contrast to the predictions of the Federal Reserve's models, unemployment rose more rapidly in 2008 and 2009 than at any time since the Great Depression. Inflation briefly spiked to 5 per cent in mid-2008, but then did something it had not done since the end of the Korean War: it turned negative, hitting minus 2 per cent in mid-2009. The financial markets threw up crisis after crisis, and could no longer be ignored by mainstream economists, despite the absence of the financial sector from their models.

Clearly, something was badly amiss. The confidence with which Lucas had dismissed the possibility of a Great Depression a mere four years earlier evaporated, and the response of economists in authority was sheer panic. Temporarily, they threw their economic models out the window, and pumped government money into the economy: they weren't about to let capitalism collapse on their watch. As then Treasury Secretary Hank Paulson put it in his memoir *On the Brink*, by late 2008, officials in the US administration had come to believe that, without decisive action by the government, the end of capitalism was indeed nigh:

> 'We need to buy hundreds of billions of assets', I said. I knew better than to utter the word trillion. That would have caused cardiac arrest. 'We need an announcement tonight to calm the market, and legislation next week,' I said.
>
> What would happen if we didn't get the authorities we sought, I was asked. 'May God help us all,' I replied. (Paulson, 2010, p. 261)

None of this would have surprised Hyman Minsky, had he lived to see it (he died in 1996), because this crisis, inexplicable as it was to the economic mainstream, was a core prediction of his contrarian vision of the economy.

Minsky worked outside the mainstream of economics, because he always regarded its foundations as unsound. Its basis was the 'Neoclassical' approach to economics that began in the 1870s with Leon Walras, who tried to show that a system of uncoordinated markets could reach what he called 'general equilibrium', with supply equal to demand in all markets. He and the other founding fathers of today's mainstream economics abstracted from many central features of the real world to make their modelling task easier. But without these features, what Paul Samuelson termed 'the Neoclassical Synthesis' could not explain the instability of capitalism, which to Minsky was an obvious feature of the real world:

> The abstract model of the neoclassical synthesis cannot generate instability. When the neoclassical synthesis is constructed, capital assets, financing arrangements that center around banks and money creation, constraints imposed by liabilities, and the problems associated with knowledge about uncertain futures are all assumed away. *For economists and policy-makers to do better we have to abandon the neoclassical synthesis.* (Minsky, 1982, p. 5, emphasis added)

Working completely outside the mainstream, and with his interest in finding out whether another Great Depression could happen, Minsky began with a sublime and profound truth: to answer the question of whether another financial crisis is possible, *you need an economic model that can generate a depression*: 'To answer these questions it is necessary to have an economic theory which makes great depressions one of the possible states in which our type of capitalist economy can find itself' (Minsky, 1982, p. xi). Mainstream models – especially DSGE models – could not do this: their default state was equilibrium rather than crisis, they were assumed to return to equilibrium after any 'exogenous shock', and they lacked a financial sector. So Minsky had to develop his own theory, which he christened the 'Financial Instability Hypothesis', and it led him to his conclusion that capitalism 'is inherently flawed'.

He willingly acknowledged that this was an extreme claim. 'Financial crises, domestic and international, have been associated with capitalism throughout its history', he noted, but these could have been historical accidents. So the fact that they have happened 'does not prove that they are inherent in capitalism – the crises of history may have been due to a combination of ignorance, human error and avoidable attributes of the financial system' (Minsky, 1969, p. 224). Minsky argued, on the contrary, that capitalism had an innate tendency to both cycles and crises. His argument focused not on capitalism's many weaknesses, but on its core strength: capitalism encourages risk-taking and optimism, which in turn leads to innovation that transforms both production and society itself. This is one of the key reasons why capitalism easily won the contest with socialism during the twentieth century: though the Soviets believed that, as Khrushchev put it, 'we will bury you', their 'supply-constrained' production model was easily outgrown and totally out-innovated by the 'demand-constrained' West (Kornai, 1979; Keen, 1995a).

However, innovation and growth generate a milieu of pervasive uncertainty: since the process of innovation itself transforms the future, there is no capacity for a rational anticipation of it. As Keynes noted, 'our knowledge of the future is fluctuating, vague and uncertain ... there is no scientific basis on which to form any calculable probability whatever. We simply do not know' (1937, p. 214). Given this reality, 'Views as to the future of the world are based upon evaluations of the past', as Minsky prosaically put it (1969, p. 227). Keynes, rather more evocatively, argued that one of the mechanisms we have adopted to cope with pervasive uncertainty is that:

> We assume that the present is a much more serviceable guide to the future than a candid examination of past experience would show it to have been hitherto. In other words, we largely ignore the prospect of future changes about the actual character of which we know nothing. (Keynes, 1937, p. 214)

This extrapolation of past conditions leads, Minsky argued, to herd behaviour in investment – and Keynes again put it brilliantly: 'Knowing that our own individual judgment is worthless, we endeavour to fall back on the judgment of the rest of the world which is perhaps better informed' (1937, p. 214). Consequently, a period of relatively tranquil growth after a preceding crisis leads capitalists to shift from being despondent about the future to having 'euphoric expectations' as the memory of the crisis recedes. 'It follows', Minsky asserted, that 'the fundamental instability of a capitalist economy is upward. The tendency to transform doing well into a speculative investment boom is the basic instability in a capitalist economy' (1977b, p. 13).

This instability would lead to recurring cycles, as Minsky's PhD supervisor Schumpeter had argued (Schumpeter, 1928, 1934), but not serious breakdowns, were it not for one other inherent feature of capitalism: private debt. In contrast to mainstream macroeconomics, which ignored private debt (Eggertsson & Krugman, 2012, pp. 1470–1), Minsky asserted that 'debt is an essential characteristic of a capitalist economy' (1977b, p. 10), because desired investment in excess of retained earnings is financed by debt (Fama & French,

1999a, 1999b, 2002). This leads to a medium-term cyclical process in capitalism which also causes a long-term tendency to accumulate too much private debt over a number of cycles.

Minsky argued therefore that both the cyclical tendencies of the economy and private debt had to play a central role in macroeconomic theory:

> The natural starting place for analyzing the relation between debt and income is to take an economy with a cyclical past that is now doing well. The inherited debt reflects the history of the economy, which includes a period in the not too distant past in which the economy did not do well. Acceptable liability structures are based upon some margin of safety so that expected cash flows, even in periods when the economy is not doing well, will cover contractual debt payments. As the period over which the economy does well lengthens, two things become evident in board rooms. Existing debts are easily validated and units that were heavily in debt prospered; it paid to lever. (Minsky, 1977b, p. 10)

A period of tranquil growth thus leads to rising expectations, and a tendency to increase leverage: as Minsky put it in his most famous sentence, 'Stability – or tranquility – in a world with a cyclical past and capitalist financial institutions is destabilizing' (1978, p. 10).

The boom gives way to bust for many reasons. The development of euphoric expectations leads to finance being given to projects that are doomed to fail, and to banks accepting 'liability structures – their own and those of borrowers – that, in a more sober expectational climate, they would have rejected', and these euphoric investments accumulate losses during the boom; the demand for finance during the boom drives up money market interest rates, reducing the financial viability of many otherwise conservative investments; stock market participants may sell equities in response to perceived excessive asset valuations at the height of a boom, thus triggering a collapse in credit (Minsky, 1982, pp. 122–4).

Another factor that Minsky did not consider, but which is a key feature of a cyclical economy (Goodwin, 1967; Blatt 1983, pp. 204–16), is that the boom will alter the distribution of income. As the economy starts to boom thanks to higher investment, employment rises, and there is greater demand for raw materials. This drives up wages and the prices of commodity inputs. Since investment in excess of retained earnings is debt-financed, the debt ratio also rises during the boom, so that debt servicing costs rise as well. These higher wage, input and interest costs ultimately mean that the profits expected by capitalists when the boom began are not realised. The increased share of output going to workers, commodity producers and bankers leaves less than capitalists had expected as profits. Investment falls, the rate of growth of the economy falters, and the boom gives way to a slump.

The slump turns euphoric expectations into depressed ones, and reverses the interest rate, asset price and income distribution dynamics that the boom set in train. Aggregate demand falls, leading to falling employment and declining wage and materials costs; but at the same time, lower cash flows after the crisis mean that actual debt servicing falls short of what was planned. The recovery from the crisis thus leaves a residue of unpaid debt, and the long period of low employment during the slump and recovery period (after a short burst of high employment during the boom) causes the inflation rate to fall over time.

The profit share of output ultimately returns to a level that once again sets off another period of euphoric expectations and high debt-financed investment, but this starts from a higher level of debt relative to GDP than before. Inequality rises as well, since with a higher level of debt, the larger share of income going to bankers leaves a lower share for workers (and raw material suppliers).

The next boom therefore sets out with a higher debt ratio, and a lower level of inflation. And so goes the next, and the next, until finally such a level of debt is taken on that falling interest rates, falling wages and lower raw material costs during the slump cannot offset the impact of debt servicing on profits. Without bankruptcy, debt would continue to compound forever, and there would be no escape. With bankruptcy, debt is reduced, but at the cost of a diminished money supply as well, and hence diminished demand. Profits do not recover, investment terminates, and the economy – in the absence of large-scale government spending – can fall into and linger in a Great Depression.

Government spending can attenuate this process, in the same fashion that an air conditioner makes the fluctuations in temperature inside a house smaller than those in the open air. Partly driven by the level of unemployment, government spending rises during a slump as unemployment increases; government revenue, based on taxation of wages and profits, falls. However, unlike firms and households, government spending is not revenue-constrained, since it is the only institution in society that 'owns its own bank' – the Central Bank. It can easily spend more than it takes back in taxes, with the difference ultimately financed by the Central

Bank's capacity to create money. Net spending by the government therefore moves in the opposite direction to the economy itself, and provides firms with cash flow that they wouldn't otherwise have, with which they can service their debts.

However, over the last forty years, Neoliberal political philosophy, which arose from a belief in the Neoclassical vision of capitalism, encouraged governments to limit their spending, and in the process to tolerate higher and higher levels of unemployment – in effect shrinking the 'air-conditioner' effect of government spending. As the reign of Neoliberal economic policies continued, and the reaction of governments to periods of higher unemployment weakened, the likelihood that a private debt crisis would trigger a substantial economic crisis grew. 'It' could therefore happen again.

Minsky's theory is compelling, but it was ignored by the economics mainstream when he first developed it, because he refused to make the assumptions that they then insisted were required to develop 'good' economic theory. Bernanke's treatment of Minsky in his *Essays on the Great Depression* is the classic illustration of this. This book collected the papers on which Bernanke based his claim to be an expert on the Great Depression – and therefore the ideal person to head the Federal Reserve.

A dispassionate observer might have expected Bernanke to have considered all major theories that attempted to explain the Great Depression, including Minsky's. Instead, this is the *entire* consideration that Bernanke gave to Minsky in that book: 'Hyman Minsky (1977a) and Charles Kindleberger (1978) have in several places argued for the inherent instability of the financial system, but in doing so have had to depart from the assumption of rational economic behavior.' A footnote adds: 'I do not deny the possible importance of irrationality in economic life; however, it seems that the best research strategy is to push the rationality postulate as far as it will go' (Bernanke, 2000, p. 43).

The mainstream has become much less dismissive of Minsky since the crisis, and also much less convinced that its microeconomically based approach to macroeconomic modelling is justified. The influential ex-president of the Minneapolis Federal Reserve, Narayana Kocherlakota, recently commented that, given how surprising the economic data of the last decade has been for mainstream economists, they have to acknowledge that 'we simply do not have a settled successful theory of the macroeconomy':

> the premise of 'serious' modeling is that macro-economic research can and should be grounded in

an established body of theory. My own view is that, after the highly surprising nature of the data flow over the past ten years, this basic premise of 'serious' modeling is wrong: we simply do not have a settled successful theory of the macroeconomy. The choices made 25–40 years ago – made then for a number of excellent reasons – should not be treated as written in stone or even in pen. By doing so, we are choking off paths for understanding the macro economy. (Kocherlakota, 2016)

A recent paper by the World Bank's chief economist Paul Romer, entitled 'The Trouble with Macroeconomics', is even more scathing. Romer describes DSGE models as being so unrealistic as to deserve the moniker 'post-real', declares that they use 'incredible identifying assumptions to reach bewildering conclusions' (2016, p. 1), and satirises them as being driven by unobservable fictions that he likens to 'phlogiston', the imaginary substance that seventeenth-century chemists used to explain combustion before the discovery of oxygen.

But the mainstream also finds it difficult to imagine an alternative to deriving macroeconomic models from microeconomic foundations. Olivier Blanchard, who was director of research at the International Monetary Fund and was once a staunch advocate of DSGE modelling, has also come to accept that DSGE models are seriously flawed: 'They are based on unappealing assumptions. Not just simplifying assumptions, as any model must, but assumptions profoundly at odds with what we know about consumers and firms.' However, at the same time, Blanchard cannot imagine any way to derive macroeconomic models except from microeconomic foundations: 'The pursuit of a widely accepted analytical macroeconomic core, in which to locate discussions and extensions, may be a pipe dream, but it is a dream surely worth pursuing . . . Starting from explicit microfoundations is clearly essential; where else to start from?' (Blanchard, 2016).

I fully agree with Blanchard that 'a widely accepted analytical macroeconomic core' is needed – and I believe that one can be created. But its foundations are not microeconomics, since, as leading mainstream mathematical economists proved over forty years ago, macroeconomics *cannot* be derived directly from microeconomics. Given the new and welcome emphasis upon realism amongst leading mainstream macroeconomists, it's also time for them to take that proof (known as the Sonnenschein–Mantel–Debreu theorem) seriously. As intuitively reasonable as the concept of micro-foundations may have once seemed, it is also simply impossible.

# 2

# Microeconomics, Macroeconomics and Complexity

Since 1976, Robert Lucas – he of the confidence that the 'problem of depression prevention has been solved' – has dominated the development of mainstream macroeconomics with the proposition that good macroeconomic theory could only be developed from microeconomic foundations. Arguing that 'the structure of an econometric model consists of optimal decision rules of economic agents' (1976, p. 13), Lucas insisted that, to be valid, a macroeconomic model had to be derived from the microeconomic theory of the behaviour of utility-maximising consumers and profit-maximising firms.

In fact, Lucas's methodological precept – that macro-level phenomena can and in fact must be derived from micro-level foundations – had been invalidated before he stated it. As long ago as 1953 (Gorman, 1953), mathematical economists posed the question of whether what microeconomic theory predicted about the behaviour of an isolated consumer applied at the level of the market. They concluded, reluctantly, that it did not:

> market demand functions need not satisfy in any way the classical restrictions which characterize consumer demand functions ... The importance of the above results is clear: strong restrictions are needed in order to justify the hypothesis that a market demand function has the characteristics of a consumer demand function. Only in special cases can an economy be expected to act as an 'idealized consumer'. The utility hypothesis tells us nothing about market demand unless it is augmented by additional requirements. (Shafer & Sonnenschein, 1993, pp. 671–2)

What they showed was that if you took two or more consumers with different tastes and different income sources, consuming two or more goods whose relative consumption levels changed as incomes rose (because some goods are luxuries and others are necessities), then the resulting market demand curves could have almost any shape at all.[1] They didn't have to slope downwards, as economics textbooks asserted they did.

This doesn't mean that demand for an actual commodity in an actual economy will fall if its price falls, rather than rise. It means instead that this empirical regularity must be due to features that the model of a single consumer's behaviour omits. The obvious candidate for the key missing feature is the distribution of income between consumers, which will change when prices change.

The reason that aggregating individual downward-sloping demand curve results in a market demand curve that can have any shape at all is simple to understand, but – for those raised in the mainstream tradition – very difficult to accept. The individual demand curve is derived by assuming that relative prices can change without affecting the consumer's income. This assumption can't be made when you consider all of society – which you must do when aggregating individual demand to derive a market demand curve – because changing relative prices will change relative incomes as well.

Since changes in relative prices change the distribution of income, and therefore the distribution of demand between different markets, demand for a good may *fall* when its price falls, because the price fall reduces the income of its customers more than the lower relative price boosts demand (I give a simple illustration of this in Keen, 2011, on pages 51–3).

The sensible reaction to this discovery is that individual demand functions can be grouped only if changing relative prices won't substantially change income distribution within the group. This is valid if you aggregate all wage earners into a group called 'Workers', all profit earners into a group called 'Capitalists', and all rent earners into a group called 'Bankers' – or in other words, if you start your analysis from the level of social classes. Alan Kirman proposed such a response almost three decades ago:

> If we are to progress further we may well be forced to theorise in terms of groups who have collectively coherent behaviour. Thus demand and expenditure functions if they are to be set against reality must be defined at some reasonably high level of aggregation. The idea that we should start at the level of the isolated individual is one which we may well have to abandon. (Kirman, 1989, p. 138)

Unfortunately, the reaction of the mainstream was less enlightened: rather than accepting this discovery, they looked for conditions under which it could be ignored. These conditions are absurd – they amount to assuming that all individuals *and all commodities* are identical. But the desire to maintain the mainstream methodology of constructing macro-level models by simply extrapolating from individual-level models won out over realism.

The first economist to derive this result, William Gorman, argued that it was 'intuitively reasonable' to make what is in fact an absurd assumption, that changing the distribution of income does not alter consumption: 'The necessary and sufficient condition quoted above is intuitively reasonable. It says, in effect, that *an extra unit of purchasing power should be spent in the same way no matter to whom it is given*' (Gorman, 1953, pp. 63–4, emphasis added). Paul Samuelson, who arguably did more to create Neoclassical economics than any other twentieth-century economist, conceded that unrelated individual demand curves could not be aggregated to yield market demand curves that behaved like individual ones. But he then asserted that a 'family ordinal social welfare function' could be derived, 'since blood is thicker than water': family members could be assumed to redistribute income between themselves '*so as to keep the "marginal social significance of every dollar" equal*' (Samuelson, 1956, pp. 10–11, emphasis added). He then blithely extended this vision of a happy family to the whole of society: 'The same argument will apply to all of society *if optimal reallocations of income can be assumed to keep the ethical worth of each person's marginal dollar equal'* (1956, p. 21, emphasis added).

The textbooks from which mainstream economists learn their craft shielded students from the absurdity of these responses, and thus set them up to unconsciously make inane rationalisations themselves when they later constructed what they believed were microeconomically sound models of macroeconomics, based on the fiction of 'a representative consumer'. Hal Varian's advanced mainstream text *Microeconomic Analysis* (first published in 1978) reassured Master's and PhD students that this procedure was valid – 'it is sometimes convenient to think of the aggregate demand as the demand of some "representative consumer" ... The conditions under which this can be done are rather stringent, but a discussion of this issue is beyond the scope of this book' (Varian, 1984, p. 268) – and portrayed Gorman's intuitively ridiculous rationalisation as reasonable:

> Suppose that all individual consumers' indirect utility functions take the Gorman form ... [where] ... the marginal propensity to consume good j *is independent of the level of income of any consumer and also constant across consumers* ... This demand function can in fact be *generated* by a representative consumer. (Varian, 1992, pp. 153–4, emphasis

added. Curiously the innocuous word 'generated' in this edition replaced the more loaded word 'rationalized' in the 1984 edition.)

It's then little wonder that, decades later, macro-economic models, painstakingly derived from microeconomic foundations – *in the false belief that it was legitimate to scale the individual up to the level of society, and thus to ignore the distribution of income* – failed to foresee the biggest economic event since the Great Depression.

So macroeconomics cannot be derived from microeconomics. But this does not mean that 'The pursuit of a widely accepted analytical macro-economic core, in which to locate discussions and extensions, may be a pipe dream', as Blanchard put it. There is a way to derive macroeconomic models by starting from foundations that all economists must agree upon. But to actually do this, economists have to embrace a concept that to date the mainstream has avoided: complexity.

The discovery that higher-order phenomena cannot be directly extrapolated from lower-order systems is a commonplace conclusion in genuine sciences today: it's known as the 'emergence' issue in complex systems (Nicolis and Prigogine, 1971; Ramos-Martin, 2003). The dominant characteristics of a complex system come from the interactions between its entities, rather than from the properties of a single entity considered in isolation.

My favourite instance of this is the behaviour of water. If one *had* to derive macroscopic behaviour from microscopic principles, then weather forecasters would *have* to derive the myriad properties of the weather from the characteristics of a single molecule of $H_2O$. This would entail showing how, under appropriate conditions, a 'water molecule' could become an 'ice molecule', a 'steam molecule', or – my personal favourite – a 'snowflake molecule'. In fact, the wonderful properties of water occur, not because of the properties of individual $H_2O$ molecules themselves, but because of interactions between lots of (identical) $H_2O$ molecules.

The fallacy in the belief that higher-level phenomena (like macroeconomics) have to be, or even could be, derived from lower-level phenomena (like microeconomics) was pointed out clearly in 1972 – again, before Lucas wrote – by the Physics Nobel Laureate Philip Anderson:

The main fallacy in this kind of thinking is that the reductionist hypothesis does not by any means imply a 'constructionist' one: *The ability to reduce*

> *everything to simple fundamental laws does not imply the ability to start from those laws and reconstruct the universe.* (Anderson, 1972, p. 393, emphasis added)

Anderson specifically rejected the approach of extrapolating from the 'micro' to the 'macro' within physics. If this rejection applies to the behaviour of fundamental particles, how much more so does it apply to the behaviour of people?

> The behavior of large and complex aggregates of elementary particles, it turns out, is not to be understood in terms of a simple extrapolation of the properties of a few particles. Instead, at each level of complexity entirely new properties appear, and the understanding of the new behaviors requires research which I think is as fundamental in its nature as any other. (Anderson, 1972, p. 393)

Anderson was willing to entertain that there was a hierarchy to science, so that 'one may array the sciences roughly linearly in a hierarchy, according to the idea: "The elementary entities of science X obey the laws of science Y"' (see Table 1). But he rejected the idea that any science in the X column could simply be treated as the applied version of the relevant science in the Y column:

But this hierarchy does not imply that science X is 'just applied Y'. At each stage entirely new laws, concepts, and generalizations are necessary, requiring inspiration and creativity to just as great a degree as in the previous one. Psychology is not applied biology, nor is biology applied chemistry. (Anderson, 1972, p. 393)

**Table 1.** Anderson's hierarchical ranking of sciences (adapted from Anderson, 1972, p. 393)

| X | Y |
| --- | --- |
| Solid state or many-body physics | Elementary particle physics |
| Chemistry | Many-body physics |
| Molecular biology | Chemistry |
| Cell biology | Molecular biology |
| . . . | . . . |
| Psychology | Physiology |
| Social sciences | Psychology |

Nor is macroeconomics applied microeconomics. Mainstream economists have accidentally proven Anderson right by their attempt to reduce macroeconomics to applied microeconomics, firstly by proving it was impossible, and secondly by ignoring this proof, and consequently developing macroeconomic models that blindsided economists to the biggest economic event of the last seventy years.

The impossibility of taking a 'constructionist' approach, as Anderson described it, to macroeconomics means that if we are to derive a decent macroeconomics, *we have to start at the level of the macroeconomy itself.* This is the approach of complex-systems theorists: to work from the structure of the system they are analysing, since this structure, properly laid out, will contain the interactions between the system's entities that give it its dominant characteristics. This was how the first complex-systems models of physical phenomena were derived: the so-called 'many-body problem' in astrophysics, and the problem of turbulence in fluid flow.

Newton's equation for gravitational attraction explained how a predictable elliptical orbit results from the gravitational attraction of the Sun and a single planet, but it could not be generalised to explain the dynamics of the multi-planet system in which we actually live. The great French mathematician Henri Poincaré discovered in 1899 that the orbits would be what we now call 'chaotic': even with a set of equations to describe their motion, accurate prediction of their future motion would require infinite precision of measurement of their positions and velocities today. As astrophysicist Scott Tremaine put it, since infinite accuracy of measurement is impossible, then 'for practical purposes the positions of the planets are unpredictable further than about a hundred million years in the future':

> As an example, shifting your pencil from one side of your desk to the other today could change the gravitational forces on Jupiter enough to shift its position from one side of the Sun to the other a billion years from now. The unpredictability of the solar system over very long times is of course ironic since this was the prototypical system that inspired Laplacian determinism. (Tremaine, 2011)

This unpredictable nature of complex systems led to the original description of the field as 'Chaos Theory', because in place of the regular cyclical patterns of harmonic systems there appeared to be no pattern at all in complex ones. A good illustration of this is Figure 1, which plots the superficially chaotic behaviour over time of two of the three variables in the complex-systems model of the weather developed by Edward Lorenz in 1963.

However, long-term unpredictability means neither a total lack of predictability, nor a lack of structure. You almost surely know of the phrase 'the butterfly effect': the saying that a butterfly flapping or not flapping its wings in Brazil can make the difference between the occurrence or not of a hurricane in China. The butterfly metaphor was

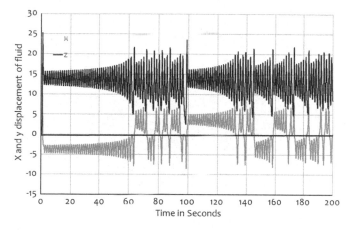

**Figure 1.** The apparent chaos in Lorenz's weather model

inspired by plotting the three variables in Lorenz's model against each other in a '3D' diagram. The apparently chaotic behaviour of the x and y variables in the '2D' plot of Figure 1 gives way to the beautiful 'wings of a butterfly' pattern shown in Figure 2 when all three dimensions of the model are plotted against each other.

The saying does not mean that butterflies cause hurricanes, but rather that imperceptible differences in initial conditions can make it essentially impossible to predict the path of complex systems like the weather after a relatively short period of time. Though this eliminates the capacity to make truly long-term weather forecasts, the capacity to forecast

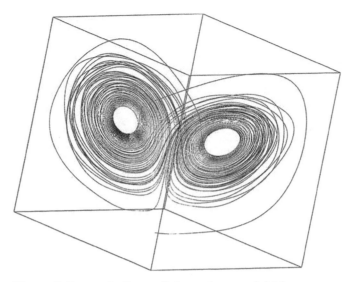

**Figure 2.** Lorenz's 'butterfly' weather model (the same data as in Figure 1 in three dimensions)

for a finite but still significant period of time is the basis of the success of modern meteorology.

Lorenz developed his model because he was dissatisfied with the linear models that were used at the time to make weather forecasts, when meteorologists knew that the key phenomena in weather involved key variables – such as the temperature and density of a gas – interacting with each other in non-additive ways. Meteorologists already had non-linear equations for fluid flow, but these were too complicated to simulate on computers in Lorenz's day. So he produced a drastically simplified model of fluid flow with just three equations and three parameters (constants) – and yet this extremely simple model developed extremely complex cycles which captured the essence of the instability in the weather itself.

Lorenz's very simple model generated sustained cycles because, for realistic parameter values, its three equilibria were all unstable. Rather than dynamics involving a disturbance followed by a return to equilibrium, as happens with stable linear models, the dynamics involved the system being far from equilibrium at all times. To apply Lorenz's insight, meteorologists had to abandon their linear, equilibrium models – which they willingly did – and develop nonlinear ones which could be simulated on computers. This has led, over the last half-century, to far more accurate weather forecasting than was possible with linear models.

The failure of economics to develop anything like the same capacity is partly because the economy is far less predictable than the weather, given human agency, as Hayekian economists justifiably argue. But it is also due to the insistence of mainstream economists on the false modelling strategies of deriving macroeconomics by extrapolation from microeconomics, and of assuming that the economy is a stable system that always returns to equilibrium after a disturbance.

Abandoning these false modelling procedures does not lead, as Blanchard fears, to an inability to develop macroeconomic models from a 'widely accepted analytical macroeconomic core'. Neoclassical macroeconomists have tried to derive macroeconomics from the wrong end – that of the individual rather than the economy – and have done so in a way that glosses over the aggregation problems that are entailed by pretending that an isolated individual can be scaled up to the aggregate level. It is certainly sounder – and may well be easier – to proceed in the reverse direction, by starting from aggregate statements that are true by definition, and then disaggregating those when more detail is required. In other words, a 'core' exists in the very definitions of macroeconomics.

Using these definitions, it is possible to develop, from first principles that no macroeconomist can dispute, a model that does four things that no DSGE model can do: it generates endogenous cycles; it reproduces the tendency to crisis that Minsky argued was endemic to capitalism; it explains the growth of inequality over the last fifty years; and it implies that the crisis will be preceded, as indeed it was, by a 'Great Moderation' in employment and inflation.

The three core definitions from which a rudimentary macro-founded macroeconomic model can be derived are 1) the employment rate (the ratio of those with a job to total population, as an indicator of both the level of economic activity and the bargaining power of workers), 2) the wages share of output (the ratio of wages to GDP, as an indicator of the distribution of income), and 3), as Minsky insisted, the private debt to GDP ratio.[2] When put in dynamic form, these definitions lead not merely to 'intuitively reasonable' statements, but to statements that are true by definition:

- The employment rate (the percentage of the population that has a job) will rise if the rate of economic growth (in per cent per year) exceeds the sum of population growth and labour productivity growth.
- The percentage share of wages in GDP will rise if wage demands exceed the growth in labour productivity.
- The debt to GDP ratio will rise if private debt grows faster than GDP.

These are simply truisms. To turn them into an economic model, we have to postulate some relationships between the key entities in the system: between employment and wages, between profit and investment, and between debt, profits and investment.

Here an insight from complex-systems analysis is extremely important: a simple model can explain most of the behaviour of a complex system, because most of its complexity comes from the fact that its components interact – and not from the well-specified behaviour of the individual components themselves (Goldenfeld and Kadanoff, 1999). So the simplest possible relationships may still reveal the core properties of the dynamic system – which in this case is the economy itself.

In this instance, the simplest possible relationships are:

- Output is a multiple of the installed capital stock.
- Employment is a multiple of output.
- The rate of change of the wage is a linear function of the employment rate.
- Investment is a linear function of the rate of profit.
- Debt finances investment in excess of profits.
- Population and labour productivity grow at constant rates.

The resulting model is far less *complicated* than even a plain vanilla DSGE model: it has just three variables, nine parameters, and no random terms.[3] It omits many obvious features of the real world, from government and bankruptcy provisions at one extreme to Ponzi lending to households by the banking sector at the other. As such, there are many features of the real world that cannot be captured without extending its simple foundations.[4]

However, even at this simple level, its behaviour is far more *complex* than even the most advanced DSGE model, for at least three reasons. Firstly, the relationships between variables in this model aren't constrained to be simply additive, as they are in the vast majority of DSGE models: changes in one variable can therefore compound changes in another, leading to changes in trends that a linear DSGE model cannot capture. Secondly, non-equilibrium behaviour isn't ruled out by assumption, as in DSGE models: the entire range of outcomes that can happen is considered, and not just those that are either compatible with or lead towards equilibrium. Thirdly, the finance sector, which is ignored in DSGE models (or at best treated merely as a source of 'frictions' that slow down the convergence to equilibrium), is included in a simple but fundamental way in this model, by the empirically confirmed assumption that investment in excess of profits is debt-financed (Fama & French, 1999a, p. 1954).[5]

The model generates two feasible outcomes, depending on how willing capitalists are to invest. A lower level of willingness leads to equilibrium. A higher level leads to crisis.

With a low propensity to invest, the system stabilises: the debt ratio rises from zero to a constant level, while cycles in the employment rate and wages share gradually converge on equilibrium values. This process is shown in Figure 3, which plots the employment rate and the debt ratio.

With a higher propensity to invest comes the debt-driven crisis that Minsky predicted, and which we experienced in 2008. However, something that Minsky did not predict, but which did happen in the

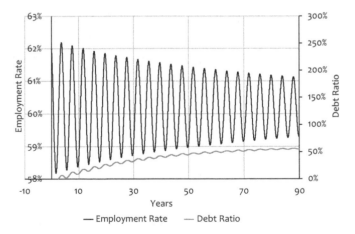

**Figure 3.** Equilibrium with less optimistic capitalists

real world, also occurs in this model: *the crisis is preceded by a period of apparent economic tranquillity* that superficially looks the same as the transition to equilibrium in the good outcome. Before the crisis begins, there is a period of diminishing volatility in unemployment, as shown in Figure 4: the cycles in employment (and wages share) diminish, and at a faster rate than the convergence to equilibrium in the good outcome shown in Figure 3.

But then the cycles start to rise again: apparent moderation gives way to increased volatility, and ultimately a complete collapse of the model, as the employment rate and wages share of output collapse to zero and the debt to GDP ratio rises to infinity.

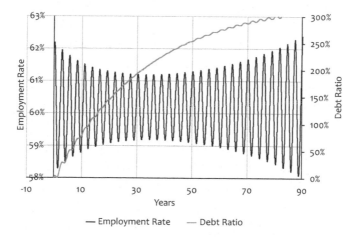

**Figure 4.** Crisis with more optimistic capitalists

This model, derived simply from the incontestable foundations of macroeconomic definitions, implies that the 'Great Moderation', far from being a sign of good economic management as mainstream economists interpreted it (Blanchard et al., 2010, p. 3), was actually a warning of an approaching crisis.

The difference between the good and bad outcomes is the factor Minsky insisted was crucial to understanding capitalism, but which is absent from mainstream DSGE models: the level of private debt. It stabilises at a low level in the good outcome, but reaches a high level and does not stabilise in the bad outcome.

The model produces another prediction which has also become an empirical given: rising inequality. Workers' share of GDP falls as the debt ratio rises, even though in this simple model workers do no borrowing at all. If the debt ratio stabilises, then inequality stabilises too, as income shares reach positive equilibrium values. But if the debt ratio continues rising – as it does with a higher propensity to invest – then inequality keeps rising as well. Rising inequality is therefore not merely a 'bad thing' in this model: it is also a prelude to a crisis.

The dynamics of rising inequality are more obvious in the next stage in the model's development, which introduces prices and variable nominal interest rates. As debt rises over a number of cycles, a rising share going to bankers is offset by a smaller share going to workers, so that the capitalists' share fluctuates but remains relatively constant over time. However, as wages and inflation are driven down, the compounding of debt ultimately overwhelms falling wages, and profit share collapses. Before this crisis ensues, the rising amount going to bankers in debt service is precisely offset by the declining share going to workers, so that profit share becomes effectively constant and the world appears utterly tranquil to capitalists – just before the system fails.

I built a version of this model in 1992, long before the 'Great Moderation' was apparent. I had

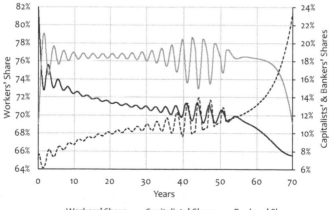

— Workers' Share — Capitalists' Share - - - Bankers' Share

**Figure 5.** Rising inequality caused by rising debt

expected the model to generate a crisis, since I was attempting to model Minsky's Financial Instability Hypothesis. But the moderation before the crisis was such a striking and totally unexpected phenomenon that I finished my paper by focusing on it, with what I thought was a nice rhetorical flourish:

> From the perspective of economic theory and policy, this vision of a capitalist economy with finance requires us to go beyond that habit of mind which Keynes described so well, the excessive reliance on the (stable) recent past as a guide to the future. *The chaotic dynamics explored in this paper should warn us against accepting a period of relative tranquility in a capitalist economy as anything other than a lull before the storm.* (Keen, 1995b, p. 634, emphasis added)

Though my model did predict that these phenomena of declining cycles in employment and inflation[6] and rising inequality would precede a crisis if one were to occur, I didn't expect my rhetorical flourish to manifest itself in actual economic data. There were, I thought, too many differences between my simple, private-sector-only model and the complicated (as well as complex) real world for this to happen.

But it did.

# 3

# The Lull and the Storm

At the time that I developed my model, the global economy was still mired in the recession that, later that year, would hand the keys to the White House to Bill Clinton, on the back of the slogan 'It's the Economy, Stupid'. Unemployment had just peaked at 7.8 per cent – a substantial level compared to the post-war average of 5.6 per cent, but nowhere near as severe as the 1983 recession, when it hit 10.8 per cent. From August 1992 on, unemployment trended down as the US economy embarked on first the telecommunications boom and then the DotCom Bubble of the 1990s. Inflation had fallen sharply from the elevated levels of the late 1970s, but as this new boom took hold, there were fears that inflation would take off once more.

It didn't: inflation trended down as unemployment fell, dropping from 3 per cent at the height of the 1990s recession to 1.5 per cent per annum in the late 1990s.

When the DotCom Bubble ended with the collapse of the Nasdaq Index in 2000, the ensuing downturn turned out to be mild. Unemployment peaked at just 6.3 per cent in mid-2003, and inflation fell to just over 1 per cent. Even before the downturn hit its nadir, mainstream Neoclassical economists observed the trend that, from their point of view, was clearly a positive one: the 'Great Moderation' (Stock & Watson, 2002).

In contrast to the orgy of self-congratulation in mainstream economics, alarms were being sounded by non-mainstream economists – and in particular by the English economist Wynne Godley (Godley & McCarthy, 1998; Godley & Wray, 2000; Godley, 2001; Godley & Izurieta, 2002, 2004; Godley et al., 2005). The key reason why Godley saw trouble looming was that he had developed a method to analyse the economy using inter-sectoral monetary flows. He applied the truism that one sector's monetary surplus must be matched by an identical deficit in other sectors to argue that the trend towards a US government surplus at the time required an unsustainable rise in private sector indebtedness.

In the provocatively titled 'Is Goldilocks Doomed?', Godley and Wray (2000) asserted that, at some point, the private sector would have to stop borrowing, and when it did, the long-running boom would give way to a severe recession. Unfortunately, Godley's warnings in this and several other equally provocative papers were ignored by politicians and the mainstream economists who advised them, for several reasons. The most important was that Godley did not make the assumptions the mainstream required: his papers discussed inter-sectoral monetary and credit flows, not the optimising behaviour of rational agents. His analysis was also strictly in terms of money stocks and flows, when the mainstream had long ago convinced itself that the macroeconomy could *and indeed should* be modelled as if money, banks and debt did not exist. As Eggertsson and Krugman conceded after the crisis, the vast majority of mainstream economic models ignored private debt completely:

> Given the prominence of debt in popular discussion of our current economic difficulties and the long tradition of invoking debt as a key factor in major economic contractions, one might have expected debt to be at the heart of most mainstream macroeconomic models – especially the analysis of monetary and fiscal policy. *Perhaps somewhat surprisingly, however, it is quite common to*

*abstract altogether from this feature of the economy.*
(Eggertsson & Krugman, 2012, pp. 1470–1, emphasis added)

Crucially, the mainstream could not see why the aggregate level of debt, or changes in its rate of growth, should have any macroeconomic significance. In so far as they had models of credit, these portrayed lending as a transfer of spending power from one agent to another, not as a means by which additional spending power was created – or when debts were repaid, destroyed. To the mainstream, the level and rate of change of private debt could only matter if there were extreme differences in the behaviour and/or circumstances of debtors and creditors. For this reason, Ben Bernanke dismissed Irving Fisher's argument that a debt-deflationary process caused the Great Depression:

The idea of debt-deflation goes back to Irving Fisher (1933). Fisher envisioned a dynamic process in which falling asset and commodity prices created pressure on nominal debtors, forcing them into distress sales of assets, which in turn led to further price declines and financial difficulties. His diagnosis led him to urge President Roosevelt to subordinate exchange-rate considerations to the need for reflation, advice that (ultimately) FDR followed.

# The Lull and the Storm

Fisher's idea was less influential in academic circles, though, because of the counterargument that debt-deflation represented no more than a redistribution from one group (debtors) to another (creditors). Absent implausibly large differences in marginal spending propensities among the groups, it was suggested, pure redistributions should have no significant macro-economic effects. (Bernanke, 2000, p. 24, emphasis added)

Even after the crisis, mainstream economists still reject out of hand arguments that the aggregate level and rate of change of debt matters. In 2013, Krugman dismissed Richard Koo's argument that the Japanese economy is balance-sheet constrained, on the basis that, for every debtor whose spending is constrained by debt, there must be a creditor whose spending is enhanced by it:

Maybe part of the problem is that Koo envisages an economy in which everyone is balance-sheet constrained, as opposed to one in which lots of people are balance-sheet constrained. I'd say that his vision makes no sense: where there are debtors, there must also be creditors, so there have to be at least some people who can respond to lower real interest rates even in a balance-sheet recession. (Krugman, 2013)

In fact, only analysts like Koo, who rejected the mainstream belief that private debt and monetary stocks and flows don't matter, warned of the crisis before it occurred (Bezemer, 2009, 2010, 2011b).[1]

I made my first warnings of an impending crisis in December 2005, as a side-effect to taking part in an Australian lawsuit over predatory lending (Keen, 2005). While drafting my report, I used the throw-away line that 'private debt to GDP ratios have been increasing exponentially in recent years', and then realised that, as an expert witness, I couldn't rely on mere hyperbole. I would need to check the data, and I expected that I would be forced to revise 'exponential' to something less dramatic.

So I plotted the Australian private debt to GDP data – and my jaw hit the floor. Describing the trend as exponential was no hyperbole: the correlation of the Australian private debt to GDP ratio from 1976 with a simple exponential function was a staggering 0.98. Surely, I thought, this trend could not continue, and when it ended, there would be a severe recession.

But was this merely an Australian phenomenon, or was it a global one? Data on private debt was very hard to collect – many countries didn't record it, and back then there was no centralised database like the one established by the BIS in 2014. So the next best thing to a global survey was to check the state of the world's biggest economy, the

USA, where fortunately data on private debt had been systematically collected by the Federal Reserve since 1952 (Copeland, 1951). While the trend was less clearly exponential, it still fitted a simple exponential function with a correlation coefficient of over 0.97.

I was now convinced that a global economic crisis was approaching, and I knew that it would take mainstream economists completely by surprise, since they paid no attention to either private debt or disequilibrium dynamics in their economic models. Since politicians relied upon mainstream

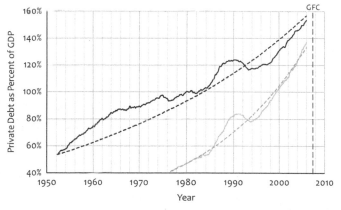

**Figure 6.** The exponential increase in debt to GDP ratios till 2006

economists for guidance about managing the economy, it was clear that the global economy was about to walk blindfolded into the greatest economic crisis in the post-war era.

My working hypothesis was that aggregate expenditure in the economy was roughly the sum of GDP plus credit, and that this sum generated both incomes (through purchases of goods and services) and realised capital gains (via net purchases of assets – predominantly property and shares). Since credit (which is equivalent to the growth in private debt) was both far more volatile than GDP and also capable of turning negative and thus subtracting from demand, the crisis would commence when the rate of growth of private debt slowed down:

> So how do I justify the stance of a Cassandra? Because things can't continue as normal, when normal involves an unsustainable trend in debt. At some point, there has to be a break – though timing when that break will occur is next to impossible, especially so when it depends in part on individual decisions to borrow ... At some point, the debt to GDP ratio must stabilise – and on past trends, it won't stop simply at stabilising. When that inevitable reversal of the unsustainable occurs, we will have a recession. (Keen 2007)

The US crisis began when my Minskian analysis indicated that it would – when the rate of growth of private debt began to slow down, and did not recover. As I explain in Chapter 4, 'The Smoking Gun of Credit', total demand in the economy – for both goods and services and assets – is the sum of the turnover of existing money plus credit (which is equivalent to the change in the level of private debt). Credit, which had averaged less than 6 per cent of GDP between 1945 and 1970, averaged 14 per cent of GDP between 2006 and 2008. Private debt had grown enormously in America over the post-war period – from just 37 per cent of GDP in 1945 to 165 per cent of GDP by 2008. A slowdown in the rate of growth of debt was inevitable, and this alone was enough to cause total demand in the economy to fall.

That slowdown began in 2008, as credit fell from plus 15 per cent of GDP at its peak, to minus 5 per cent of GDP at its nadir (see Figure 7). Credit, which had been positive for the entire post-war period and adding to demand, was now negative and subtracting from it – something that had not happened since the Great Depression. Using GDP plus credit as a rough guide to total demand in the economy, total demand fell from a peak of about $16 trillion in 2008 to a low of $13.5 trillion in 2010.

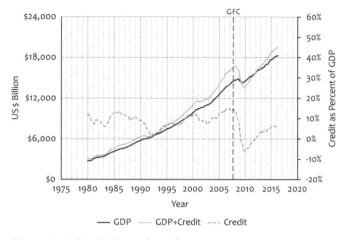

**Figure 7.** USA GDP and credit

The crash in credit-based growth caused an explosion in unemployment, and a collapse in asset prices. In contrast to the mainstream belief that changes in debt are 'pure redistributions' which 'should have no significant macro-economic effects' (Bernanke, 2000, p. 24), the change in debt was by far the major determinant of the level of unemployment, which rose dramatically as the rate of growth of private debt plummeted (see Figure 8).

The US crisis was heralded, of course, by the bursting of its house price bubble. In June of 2005, when then Federal Reserve Chairman Alan Greenspan testified to Congress that there was

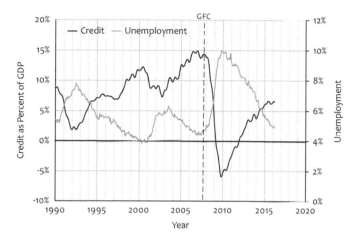

Figure 8. USA change in debt drives unemployment (correlation coefficient -0.928)

no nationwide bubble but merely 'signs of froth in some local markets' (Greenspan, 2005), even a casual inspection of the countrywide data made it obvious that America was riding the biggest bubble that it had ever experienced (see Figure 9). Though Greenspan could not have known that his ridiculous claim would coincide with the peak of the market, the fact that it did should be his final epitaph. He was a maestro of delusion, not of insight.

The bubble was driven by another factor that Greenspan and the economics mainstream also ignored: the dramatic increase in mortgage debt during the first five years of the new millennium.

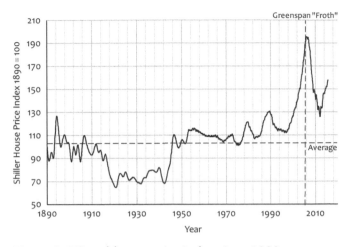

**Figure 9.** US real house price index since 1890

Mortgage debt rose from 45 per cent of GDP in 2000 to 65 per cent when Greenspan saw 'froth', and then peaked at 75 per cent of GDP before plummeting.

Here the dynamics of debt have an additional sting, since change in house prices is driven not by the level of mortgage debt, nor even by its rate of change, but by its acceleration. The logic is simple. The physical supply of housing is the turnover of existing houses, plus the net flow of newly built properties onto the market. The monetary demand for housing is fundamentally the flow of new mortgages, which is the change in the level of mortgage debt. Divide this by the current price level, and you have how many houses can be bought at the current price level. This creates a relationship between the *change* in mortgage debt and the *level* of house prices. There is therefore a relationship between the *acceleration* of mortgage debt and the *change* in house prices. Though it's a complex, nonlinear, positive feedback process, accelerating mortgage debt is in the driver's seat – and as many Americans found out to their great cost, decelerating mortgage debt causes falling house prices, and this deceleration sets in well before mortgage debt peaks.[2] This was what took the wind out of the US house price bubble, starting in 2005 – just as Greenspan was assuring Congress that there was no bubble (see Figure 10).

The American economy thus followed Minsky's script in its entirety. But a crisis did *not* occur in my home country of Australia, despite very similar data on private debt. Instead, it was one of just two OECD nations to avoid a recession during the Global Financial Crisis (the GFC; the other country that avoided a recession was South Korea). Was this a sign that Minsky's thesis doesn't apply Down Under – or in the Pacific?

This was the conventional wisdom in Australia, where Australia's Central Bank (the Reserve Bank

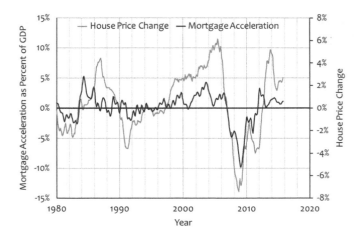

**Figure 10.** Mortgage debt acceleration and house price change

of Australia or RBA) took to referring to the 2008 crisis as the 'North Atlantic Economic Crisis' rather than the 'Global Financial Crisis', to emphasise that 'it didn't happen here' (Stevens, 2011). However, Australia did not avoid the crisis: it merely postponed it by restarting its housing bubble – twice.

Australia countered the GFC with immediate and effective discretionary government policy, following the advice of its then Treasury Secretary Ken Henry to 'Go hard, go early, and go households' (Grattan, 2010). Several of these interventions – such as boosting government spending so that firms which otherwise might go bankrupt would instead have their cash flows underwritten by a government deficit, and providing a direct cash grant to taxpayers to boost household spending (the very first instance of 'helicopter money') – were ones that Minsky had recommended.

But the key government policy that enabled Australia to postpone its crisis was to entice Australians back into its already inflated housing market, via a dramatic increase in an already generous government grant to first home buyers. Known as the 'First Home Owners Grant' or FHOG, this scheme gave first home buyers a grant of A\$7,000 towards their purchase – at a time when the average house price in Australia's capital cities was \$450,000 (Pink, 2009, p. 11). In what it described as the 'First Home Owners Boost' – and which I nicknamed the 'First Home Vendors Boost' – the Federal Government doubled this grant to \$14,000 for the purchase of an existing dwelling, and trebled it to \$21,000 for the purchase of a new dwelling. State Governments added their own bonuses on top, with the outstanding example being the State Government of Victoria, which gave another \$14,000 for the purchase of a new property outside the State capital.

With banks willing to provide a loan to a buyer with a 5 per cent deposit, this grant meant that first home buyers did not need to have any savings of their own to qualify for a mortgage. First home buyers flocked into the market, thus stopping the decline of mortgage debt in its tracks, and restarting the then faltering Australian housing bubble. House prices fell during 2008 before the scheme was started, but then rose past their pre-crisis peak until the scheme ended in mid-2010.

By then, Australia was benefiting from another bubble: the incredible increase in demand from China, driven partly by its continued industrialisation drive, but significantly also by a credit bubble that was the Chinese government's response to the GFC. So just as the Australian household sector started to de-lever, the corporate sector embarked on a borrowing spree to finance the investment in mines, ports and railways needed to satisfy what at the time was thought to be an insatiable Chinese demand for Australian coal and iron ore. These two overlapping trends in private debt meant that though the rate of growth of private debt slowed down in Australia at the time of the GFC, it never turned negative as it did in the USA. Private credit thus continued to stimulate the Australian economy, and the stimulus increased as the housing bubble and the minerals boom accelerated from 2010 on.

As that double-barrelled boom gathered steam, a remarkable thing happened: much to the amazement of Australia's Central Bank, inflation did *not* rise. The RBA had been the last Central Bank in the world to realise that a crisis was afoot in 2008, and it continued to increase its reserve interest rate until March of 2008, fighting the non-existent menace of inflation. It did not start cutting rates until August of 2008 – fully a year after the GFC began. Cementing its status as the most out-of-touch Central Bank on the planet, it was then the first to start raising rates after the GFC – in the false belief that inflation remained the primary enemy of economic stability.

The facts begged to differ, and at the end of 2011 the RBA reluctantly reversed direction once more. Its change of direction was partially motivated by the hope that lower rates would cause a resurgence in the housing market, since the Chinese export bounty had proven to be less long-lived than expected.

Australian households, faced with declining returns on bonds and a volatile stock market, duly took the RBA's lead, and in early 2012 began to pile into the housing market once more – this time not as first home buyers, but as 'investors'. Mortgage debt, which had been falling as a percentage of GDP since the termination of the First Home Vendors' Boost, started to rise again, and by the middle of 2012 house prices began to rise once more. As of 2016, Australia's inflation-adjusted house price level was 2.8 times higher than in 1986, versus a peak real price level in the USA of just under twice the 1986 level (the USA fell to 1.2 times its 1986 level after the subprime bust).

With rising household debt thrown on top of rising corporate debt, Australia returned to the exponential trajectory in its private debt to GDP ratio that had been so rudely interrupted by the GFC (see Figure 11).

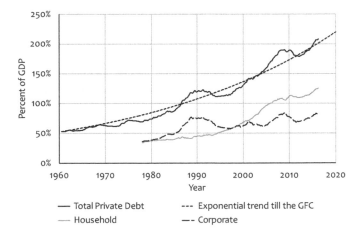

**Figure 11.** Australia's private debt to GDP ratio continues to grow exponentially

The contrast between Australia and the USA is stark. The GFC broke the exponential trend for America's private debt to GDP ratio, and though private debt is rising once more, it is rising at nothing like the rate it was prior to the crisis – and nor should it. Though America has not de-levered by anywhere near enough to enable a return to sustained growth, its private debt ratio in March 2016 was 149 per cent of GDP, 13 per cent lower than at the time of the GFC (see Figure 12). As of March 2016, Australia's private debt to GDP ratio was 208 per cent, 22 per cent *higher* than at the time of the GFC.

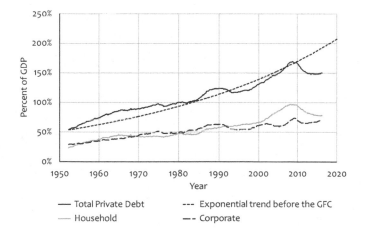

**Figure 12.** GFC breaks the exponential trend in US private debt to GDP ratio

Australia is thus the counterpoint to the USA, which shows that you can avoid a debt crisis today only by putting it off till later. The same debt dynamics that propelled and then crashed the US economy and its housing market are at work Down Under; the calamity of a debt deflation has simply been delayed by continued borrowing. When the slowdown in private debt growth begins in Australia, the fall in demand engendered by falling credit will be substantially more severe than it would have been had Australia not borrowed its way out of trouble in 2008.

Of course, you may think that it could be possible for the Australian trend of ever-rising private debt to GDP ratio to continue indefinitely. Why does private debt have to stop growing faster than GDP?

I have a one-word answer for you: Japan.

There was a time when it seemed inevitable that Japan would do with sheer economic might what it had failed to do with military muscle in the Second World War. At the end of the 1980s, nine of the world's ten biggest banks were Japanese; Japanese technology, from the Sony Walkman to the Toyota Lexus, led the world; and in 1993 – somewhat late in the piece – Hollywood released a thriller with the ominous title of *The Rising Sun*.

But as the 1990s progressed, this vision of Japanese ascendancy faded. The Nikkei Index crashed at the very beginning of the decade, Japan's booming housing market tanked shortly after, and the country entered what it came to describe as the 'Lost Decade' – a 'decade' which has now persisted for a quarter-century. Today, no Japanese bank ranks in the world's top ten (though three of Australia's four banks do); Japanese technology is still influential, but Apple and Tesla now rule where Sony and Toyota were once ascendant; and Japan now features in popular culture as a cautionary tale about fading stars, rather than rising suns.

Many explanations of Japan's malaise have been proffered by mainstream economists, from demographic decline to out-of-control government spending. A quarter of a century after its crisis began, the focus of conventional criticism today is overwhelmingly on its astronomical level of government debt, which has risen from 60 per cent to 220 per cent of GDP since its crisis began. But the real cause of Japan's sudden fall from grace was a private debt trap, just like the one that America blindly stumbled into eighteen years later.

Japan always had a high private debt to GDP ratio, largely because its Keiretsu system of interlocking ownership between industrial conglomerates and banks meant that debt from those banks played a much larger role in financing corporate investment than it did in the USA: from 1965 till 1982, the corporate debt to GDP ratio in Japan averaged 100 per cent of GDP, versus 42 per cent in the United States. Then the bubble that resulted in the 1.3 square miles of the Imperial Palace in Tokyo having a notional value similar to that of California took off. Banks provided finance not simply for technology and industry, but for share and property speculation as well, in what Japan happily labelled its 'Bubble Economy' period. Corporate debt rose by 40 per cent of GDP in just eight years.

Household debt, which had been growing rapidly but linearly (as a percentage of GDP) since 1965, also accelerated in the late 1980s, and rose by almost 25 per cent of GDP across the decade. The combination of ballooning corporate and household debt drove Japan's asset markets into the stratosphere: real house prices in Japan rose by 48 per cent from 1985 till their peak in 1991, and the Nikkei quadrupled in less than six years.

Then, at the end of the 1980s, Japan's debt-fuelled party ended. Credit, which had risen from 12 per cent of GDP in 1985 to 27 per cent in 1990, began a plunge that by the end of the 1990s saw private debt falling at up to 13 per cent of GDP per year. The result was a collapse in aggregate demand, crashing asset prices, and, crucially for

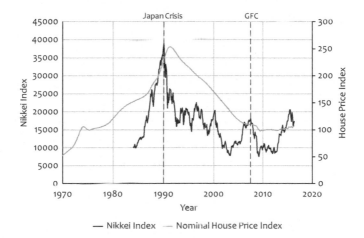

**Figure 13.** Japanese asset prices crashed when its debt-fuelled Bubble Economy ended

the once Land of the Rising Sun, the end of debt-financed investment in new technologies. Japan's major corporations were too busy attempting to repair their bloated balance sheets to invest, and the sun abruptly set on Japan's nascent economic empire. The same dynamics that would play out in America eighteen years later then ensued. Despite Japan's enormous trade surpluses and the huge compensating stimulus from rising government debt once the crisis commenced, demand in Japan stagnated and unemployment rose.

Crucially for the many countries that have since emulated Japan's pattern of a Bubble Economy followed by a crisis, private debt in Japan stabilised at a still-high level after the crisis, and demand from credit terminated. When credit stopped growing, so did Japan. The Japanese economy failed to revive after the crisis because, with the level of debt already so high, there was precious little appetite for a return to debt growth, and precious little capacity to borrow more either – even with reserve interest rates of zero. With credit either falling or negative, a vital source of demand in the Japanese economy disappeared, while every attempt to reduce debt by conventional means – by debt repayment or bankruptcy – reduced expenditure by as much,

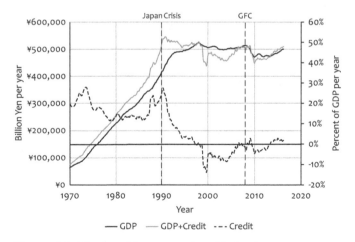

**Figure 14.** The smoking gun of credit for Japan

leaving the ratio of private debt to GDP stuck at a debilitatingly high level.

As Figure 14 shows, Japan's crisis commenced in 1990 because that was when the credit that fuelled the Bubble Economy years ceased growing, and ultimately turned negative. In the whodunnit of 'What killed the Japanese economy in 1990?', Figure 14 is the smoking gun of credit.

# 4

# The Smoking Gun of Credit

You might wonder how economists trying to understand Japan's sudden transition from economic powerhouse to economic basket case could miss as stark a piece of evidence as Figure 14. The reason is that they did not even consider this data when they went looking for clues. Their approach to sleuthing has more in common with Peter Sellers and his comic invention, the bumbling detective Inspector Clouseau, than it has with Sir Arthur Conan Doyle and Sherlock Holmes. Through a series of plausible but false propositions, they have blinded themselves to the obvious.

The original false proposition, which is drummed into students of economics in their first year at university, is that money is just a 'veil over barter', and that anyone who believes that changes in money magnitudes cause changes in 'real' magnitudes – the physical amounts of commodities that are produced and consumed in the economy – is suffering from 'money illusion'. Mainstream macroeconomics text-books confidently assure fledgling economists that absolute prices don't matter, and therefore neither does money: all that really matters are relative prices.

Rookie economic detectives are persuaded to this view by being asked to consider a consumer who has purchased a particular bundle of goods, and then asked what would change if all prices and her income were instantly doubled. 'Why, nothing sir – she would still buy the same bundle of goods' is the correct answer – and any quibbling will have you derided as suffering from 'money illusion'. From then on, mainstream models of the economy are couched in terms of relative prices rather than mon-etary ones, and money itself disappears from the analysis. In the hands of true believers like Robert Lucas, the 'absence of money illusion on the part of firms and consumers' results in an approach to macroeconomics that rules out any role for money, apart from causing inflation:

> It is natural (to an economist) to view the cyclical correlation between real output and prices as aris-ing from a volatile aggregate demand schedule that traces out a relatively stable, upward-sloping supply curve. This point of departure leads to something of

> a paradox, since *the absence of money illusion on the part of firms and consumers* appears to imply a vertical aggregate supply schedule, which in turn *implies that aggregate demand fluctuations of a purely nominal nature should lead to price fluctuations only.* (Lucas, 1972, p. 52, emphasis added)

Having eliminated money as a potential clue in any economic murder mystery, the next step in the mainstream economics detective manual is to write banks out of the script as well. Banks, it is asserted, are simply 'intermediaries' between savers and borrowers: they play no active role in either lending or money creation. The key proposition is that there is no link between lending and the amount of money in the economy: the level of debt and the amount of money are two independent things: 'Think of it this way: when debt is rising, it's not the economy as a whole borrowing more money. It is, rather, a case of less patient people – people who for whatever reason want to spend sooner rather than later – borrowing from more patient people' (Krugman, 2012a, p. 147).

The corollary of this position is the one made by Bernanke when rejecting Fisher's debt-deflation explanation for the Great Depression: that there is no link either between lending and changes in aggregate demand. Lending – even by banks – simply transfers spending power from one agent to another. Paul Krugman put this view forcefully in a blog debate with me in 2012, accusing those who argue that banks are more than intermediaries of being 'banking mystics':

> banking is where left and right meet. – Both Austrians . . . and Minskyites view banks as institutions that are somehow outside the rules that apply to the rest of the economy, as having unique powers for good and/or evil. . . – I guess I don't see it that way. Banks don't create demand out of thin air any more than anyone does by choosing to spend more; and banks are just one channel linking lenders to borrowers. (Krugman 2012c)

This argument sits rather uneasily with the third pillar of the mainstream model of money, the 'money multiplier' model of money creation; but as befuddled detectives, mainstream economists are quite capable of holding two contradictory views at once.

The money multiplier model asserts that banks *do* in fact create money by lending, but in doing so, all they are doing is passively responding to government controls. In the model, the government creates reserve money for the banks, and the banks then hold on to a fraction of this – known as the 'Required Reserve Ratio' or RRR – and lend out the rest. Borrowers then deposit this newly created money at other banks, who repeat the process until ultimately the amount of new money created equals the original creation of reserves divided by the RRR.

Since the RRR is substantially less than 1 – in America's case, it is 10 per cent (O'Brien, 2007, p. 52) – the amount of money created by bank lending, according to this model, is a multiple of the amount of reserves created by the government. So though banks do in fact create money, it's the government's fault if too much – or too little – money is created, since the government is pulling the strings. This was the basis for Bernanke's allegation that the Great Depression was caused by the Federal Reserve (2000, p. 153),[1] and also the basis of the advice President Obama followed in 2009, that the best way to rescue the economy from the GFC was not to give money to the public directly, but to give it to the banks instead (Obama, 2009).[2]

As plausible as mainstream economists find these propositions, they are both fallacious.

The first proposition, that doubling all prices and all incomes won't change any 'real' magnitudes – by which economists mean the quantity of goods and services produced and consumed in the economy – doesn't survive even casual scrutiny, once you accept the undeniable fact that debt exists.

Given that debt exists, some 'agents' will be debtors, and others will be creditors (it doesn't matter whether this involves bank debt or debt between non-bank agents). When you 'double all income and all prices', what do you do to the price of money – the interest rate? It is the cost of money for debtors, but an income source for creditors.[3] If you double it, then you make debtors worse off and creditors better off – and with this change in the distribution of income, there *will* be changes in demand and therefore in output: real magnitudes in the economy *will* change. A change in money prices and money income therefore can and does have 'real effects'. So those who assert that monetary changes will have real effects aren't suffering from 'money illusion'. Instead mainstream economists are suffering from 'barter illusion': the false belief that capitalism can be analysed without considering money at all.

The arguments that banks are 'mere intermediaries' between savers and borrowers, that there is no link between bank lending and the money supply, and that banks simply 'multiply up' central bank money to create new loans and deposits were all recently debunked by no less than the Bank of England, in the paper 'Money Creation in the Modern Economy':

In the modern economy, most money takes the form of bank deposits. But how those bank deposits are created is often misunderstood: the principal way is through commercial banks making loans. *Whenever a bank makes a loan, it simultaneously creates a matching deposit in the borrower's bank account, thereby creating new money.*

The reality of how money is created today differs from the description found in some economics textbooks:

- Rather than banks receiving deposits when households save and then lending them out, bank lending creates deposits.
- In normal times, the central bank does not fix the amount of money in circulation, nor is central bank money 'multiplied up' into more loans and deposits. (McLeay et al., 2014, p. 1, original emphasis)

The Bank's factual statement that '*Whenever a bank makes a loan, it simultaneously creates a matching deposit in the borrower's bank account, thereby creating new money*' leads to a vital corollary: money is borrowed into existence in order to be spent – either on goods and services or on assets – and that spending adds to aggregate expenditure over and above that financed by the turnover of existing money. Total demand in the economy is thus the sum of the turnover of existing money, plus credit.[4]

This is the logic behind Figure 14. To accurately measure gross expenditure, you need to add the turnover of existing money to credit. There is data on credit, but there is no data on the turnover of existing money. What is recorded is GDP – aggregate expenditure on and income from selling goods and services – which is financed partly by the turnover of existing money, and partly by credit. However, since today the vast majority of credit finances asset purchases (which are not recorded in GDP), the sum of GDP and credit *roughly* measures total expenditure in an economy.

This also explains why the level of private debt matters, as well as its rate of change. The American philanthropist Richard Vague identified a significant empirical regularity that every economic crisis over the last 150 years has manifested: the combination of a private debt to GDP ratio of 150 per cent or more, and an increase in that ratio over a five-year period of 17 per cent or more (Vague, 2014). The reason for this empirical regularity is that the impact of a slowdown in the rate of growth of debt depends on both its level and its rate of change.

To appreciate this, imagine an economy where private debt is growing twice as fast as GDP – debt is growing at 20 per cent per annum in nominal terms, and GDP is growing at 10 per cent – and where credit is 100 per cent used for asset purchases, rather than for goods and services. Ignore for the moment any feedback between credit and GDP growth. What happens to aggregate expenditure on goods and services and assets if the rate of growth of debt simply slows down to the same as the rate of growth of GDP?

If GDP is 1 trillion dollars a year, and the debt ratio is 50 per cent, then debt is $500 billion and credit that year is $100 billion (20 per cent of $500 billion). Total expenditure is $1.1 trillion: $1 trillion from the turnover of existing money, and $100 billion from credit. Next year, if GDP grows by 10 per cent, and debt growth slows down from 20 per cent a year to 10 per cent, total demand will be $1.16 trillion: $1.1 trillion from GDP, and $60 billion from credit (10 per cent of $600 billion). This is $40 billion less demand from credit than the year before, but overall demand is $60 billion higher than in the previous year, because of the increase in GDP.

However, if the debt ratio starts at 200 per cent of GDP, then total expenditure in the first year is $1.4 trillion – $1 trillion from the turnover of existing money and $400 billion from credit (20 per cent of $2 trillion). When the growth of credit slows to 10 per cent the following year, total demand is $1.34 trillion: $1.1 trillion from GDP, and $240 billion from credit (10 per cent of $2.4 trillion). This is $60 billion *less* expenditure than the year beforehand – even though both GDP and debt have continued to grow.

So the hope that I have seen some Central Bank economists express, that the level of private debt to GDP can stabilise without any ill effects on the economy, is simply false. Once an economy has a substantial level of private debt to GDP, and that ratio is growing faster than GDP, then a stabilisation of the ratio will cause a serious recession, *even without any reduction in the rate of GDP growth*. And of course in practice GDP growth does drop – hence the empirical regularity found by Vague can occur at lower levels than in this hypothetical example.

So credit is the cause of both the booms and the slumps of the global economy, and its smoking gun can be found at the scene of every economic crisis – even ones like in Spain and Greece where the suicidal policies of the Eurozone are a key additional cause of economic failure. The recent declines in the unemployment rates in southern Europe, which are being touted by the European Union as signs of the success of its austerity policies, are in fact the consequence of an increase in credit – even though it is still negative, its slower rate of decline has meant an increase in aggregate demand.

Credit has thus been a serial 'Zombifier' of economies, turning once vibrant economies into the 'Walking Dead of Debt' after exciting but unsustainable booms. These 'Debt Zombies' are characterised by a very high level of private debt (more than 150 per cent of GDP) and credit-based demand before the crisis (equivalent to about 15 per cent of GDP), and a still-high debt ratio after the crisis, but low to negative credit-based demand. With credit-based demand much lower after the crisis than before it, and private debt still stubbornly high, demand is lower, the growth rates of their economies are lower, and they are susceptible to any return to deleveraging by the private sector.

This is the real cause of the post-GFC economic stagnation that Larry Summers has, like Alvin Hansen before him, wrongly termed 'secular stagnation' (Hansen, 1934, 1939; Summers, 2014). As a mainstream economist, Summers shares the delusion that the financial crisis was a transitory phenomenon which has been resolved, and which therefore cannot explain today's desultory growth figures:

It has now been more than five years ... since evidence of systemic financial risk ... has been pervasive. Yet US economic growth has averaged only 2% over the last 5 years, despite having started from a highly depressed state. . .

Upon reflection, these patterns should be surprising. *If a financial crisis represents a kind of power failure, one would expect growth to accelerate after its resolution* as those who could not express demand because of a lack of credit were enabled to do so. (Summers, 2014, p. 30, emphasis added)

Blinded to a 'credit-and-excessive-private-debt' explanation for today's economic doldrums, Summers argues firstly that the 'zero lower bound' on interest rates has prevented the market restoring full employment:

How might one understand why growth would remain anaemic *in the absence of major financial concerns?* Suppose that a substantial shock ... tended to raise private saving propensities and reduce investment propensities . . . one would expect interest rates to fall ... until the saving and investment rate were equated at the full-employment level of output ... But this presupposes full flexibility of interest rates ... Hence the possibility exists that no attainable interest rate will permit the balancing of saving and investment at full employment. (Summers, 2014, pp. 31–2, emphasis added)

Secondly, he surmises that a slowdown in population growth and innovation explains the lower rate of growth of the economy: 'Slower population and possibly technological growth means a reduction in the demand for new capital goods to equip new or more productive workers' (2014, p. 33). Population growth has indeed slowed, and this does reduce the maximum potential growth rate of output. But the assertion that technological growth *per se* has declined is as convincing today as it was when Hansen claimed the same in 1934 (1934, p. 11) – before the invention of the jet aircraft, digital computers and atomic power.[5] The real cause in any decline in realised technical change is the same as the real cause of the slowdown in economic growth: the evaporation of credit demand, and with it the decline of a major source of finance for innovation by the private sector.

Contrary to Summers' assumption, the USA's financial crisis is not over, because the level of private debt has remained high. Private debt has fallen just 21 per cent from its peak of 170 per cent of GDP in early 2009, and it is on the cusp of the 150 per cent of GDP level that Richard Vague identified as one of the two ingredients for all past economic crises. In contrast, private debt fell substantially after the Great Depression and the Second World War, and when the post-war era began, it was just 37 per cent of GDP – a quarter of its peak level during the Great Depression.

Because private debt remains high, credit-based demand has fallen dramatically, from 12 per cent of GDP for the five years before the GFC to just 3 per cent of GDP on average from 2011 till now. Here the USA repeated the mistake Japan made eighteen years earlier, by letting private debt run rampant and ignoring asset bubbles, and then failing to reduce private debt substantially after the crisis.

Japan became the first Debt Zombie when its Bubble Economy crashed in 1990, with its private debt at 208 per cent of GDP. Credit averaged 17.5 per cent of GDP for the five years before the crisis, but under 0.5 per cent of GDP since. Private debt has fallen substantially from its peak – from 221 per cent of GDP in 1995 to 167 per cent today – but it is still well above Japan's pre-Bubble Economy level, and it has been stubbornly frozen at about 170 per cent of GDP for over a decade.

In addition to the USA, several other countries joined Japan in this Zombified state, by repeating

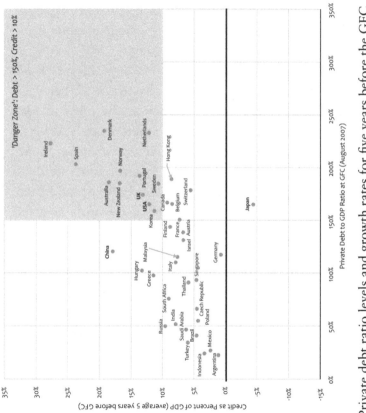

**Figure 15.** Private debt ratio levels and growth rates for five years before the GFC

its dubious formula. Figure 15 shows the private debt ratio for every country in the BIS database at the time of the GFC, and average credit levels for the five years before that date. The danger zone is the top right-hand quadrant of the graph, where private debt exceeds 150 per cent of GDP and credit is of the order of 10 per cent or more of GDP for the preceding five years. There were only two means of escape for any country that got itself into this predicament (ignoring for the moment the third option of sensible government policy): either delay the crisis by taking on yet more debt, and move further into the danger zone; or collapse out of the danger zone via a crisis that drastically reduces credit demand for evermore.

In alphabetical order, the other countries that became Debt Zombies in 2008 in addition to the USA are Denmark, Ireland, the Netherlands, New Zealand, Portugal, Spain and the UK. The average private debt level for these seven countries at the time of the GFC was 207 per cent of GDP, and credit for the five years before the crisis averaged 18 per cent of GDP. Since the crisis, their debt levels have fallen only marginally to 204 per cent of GDP on average, and credit over the last five years has averaged *minus* 1 per cent.

However, though the collapse of credit is the real

cause of their economic slowdowns, the political narrative in each country has identified a different culprit. The standard practice has been to describe a major symptom of the crisis – the blowout in government spending – as its cause. Nowhere has this diversionary tactic been more successful than in the UK.[6]

The great political success of the UK's Conservative Party has been to convince the voting public, much of the media, and even its primary political opponent the Labour Party, that the UK's recession in 2008 was caused by the deficits run by the then Labour government. The Conservative Party's 2015 manifesto described Britain's recession in 2008 as 'Labour's Great Recession', and alleged that the economy recovered because the Conservative government had halved the deficit since coming to office:

Five years ago, Britain was reeling from the chaos of Labour's Great Recession; in 2014 we were the fastest growing of all the major advanced economies . . . Five years ago, the budget deficit was more than 10 per cent of GDP, the highest in our peacetime history, and the national debt was rising out of control; today, the deficit is half that level and debt as a share of national income will start falling this financial year. (Conservative Party, 2015)

Rather than challenging this narrative – by, for example, pointing out that 2008 recession was a global phenomenon, and therefore it could not be the fault of the UK government alone – the Labour Party accepted it. Its 2015 election manifesto repeated, *ad nauseam*, that it would, if re-elected, 'cut the deficit every year':

> A Labour government *will cut the deficit every year*. The first line of Labour's first Budget will be: 'This Budget *cuts the deficit every year*.' This manifesto sets out that we will only lay a Budget before the House of Commons that *cuts the deficit every year*, which the OBR will independently verify.
>
> We will get national debt falling and *a surplus on the current budget* as soon as possible in the next parliament. This manifesto sets out that we will not compromise on this commitment. (Labour Party, 2015, emphasis added)

This was not an election manifesto: it was a confession of guilt. But in fact the only thing the Blair/Brown Labour government was guilty of was being in office when the staggering trend in UK private debt growth since 1981 broke down.

Just how unsustainable that trend was has only become obvious since the crisis, thanks to the Bank of International Settlements, and the Bank of England via its publication 'The UK Recession in Context – What Do Three Centuries of Data Tell Us?' (Hills et al., 2010). What that data tells us, most emphatically, is that the bubble in private debt in the UK between 1980 and 2008 was historically unprecedented. Private debt, which had never exceeded 75 per cent of GDP in England's history, rose from 60 per cent of GDP in the late 1970s to 127 per cent of GDP by 1991, and then a peak level of 197 per cent of GDP in mid-2009.

Therefore, if any politician deserves the blame for the 2008 recession, it was not Gordon Brown but Margaret Thatcher. Shortly after her term as prime minister began, the private debt to GDP ratio, which had shown no trend for the century before her, began to climb at three times the rate that it was rising in the USA (see Figure 16). Thatcher's championing of financial deregulation unleashed not capitalist innovation, but speculative lending by the City of London, which rode this rocket of debt to become the dominant economic and political force in the UK (and set off London's housing bubble, which bedevils UK society to this day).

This climb had to end, and by the time it peaked, the debt ratio had reached 3.3 times the 1980 level. In contrast, the private debt ratio in the USA when its debt level peaked was 'only' 1.75 times its 1980

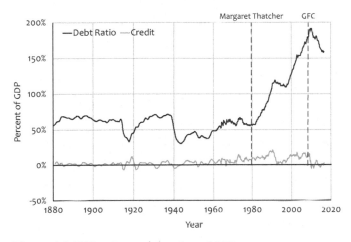

**Figure 16.** UK private debt since 1880

level. The UK's sum of GDP plus credit peaked in March 2008, and began to fall in April 2008. This is also the official date for the start of the UK's 2008 recession.

Far from the UK government deficit causing the 2008 recession, it – and similarly expanded government deficits around the world (even in Germany) – softened the blow from the collapse in credit-financed demand. The increase in government spending at the time of the crisis was largely built into the UK's fiscal system: with government revenue based largely on income tax, and government spending largely determined by the level of unemployment, declining tax receipts and rising unemployment drove the government into a larger deficit. The causal link thus runs from credit to employment, and from employment to government spending – not vice versa. Government debt, which had generally been falling as a share of GDP from the end of the Second World War, rose as a consequence of the collapse in credit-based demand.

Rising government spending in turn attenuated the severity of the economic downturn – as it had done earlier in Japan. Government spending provided firms and households with an alternative source of cash flow with which private debt could be serviced. Without it – as was the case in the Great Depression, and as is the case now in the Eurozone – unemployment would have been dramatically higher. With it, unemployment still rose, but not to the crushing levels of the Great Depression, or of the Maastricht Treaty-inspired strangulation of southern Europe today.

Now, in the aftermath to its debt bubble, credit demand in Britain is anaemic. This, and not the government deficit, is the reason that the UK economy is effectively becalmed.

There are still quite a few economies today where growth is being stimulated by credit. But many of these will experience their 'Minsky moment' and join the Walking Dead of Debt in the next few years, right under the noses of the Inspector Clouseaus of most Central Banks, who continue to ignore the role of private debt in economies. These future 'Debt Zombies' are countries where private debt levels are high, and where it is still rising much faster than nominal GDP. They have become highly dependent on credit to sustain current levels of demand and income, and when credit falls their domestic demand will plummet and their economies will enter recessions. This will affect the rest of the world as well, since that part of their demand for imports which is credit-based will disappear. While none of these countries are as significant as America in terms of their percentage of global GDP, the most significant (China) is more than half the USA's size, and collectively they are equivalent to the USA.

Picking the precise timing of a debt crisis is impossible, since, as Australia showed in 2008, a crisis can be put off for a decade if the private sector can be enticed to continue borrowing. But as Australia also demonstrates, this inevitably leads to even more leverage. Since this can't go on forever, a crisis is inevitable. The indicators of (a) the debt to GDP ratio and (b) average credit over the last five years make it easy to identify countries that are liable to face a future debt crisis. These are the countries in the upper right-hand quadrant of Figure 17, which updates Figure 15 to March 2016, the latest date for which data was available when this book was completed in September 2016.

The outstanding candidates for future Debt Zombies are Ireland, Hong Kong and China.[7] The others which have both requisites for a debt crisis – a high level of debt, and a substantial reliance on credit as a source of demand for the last half-decade – are (in alphabetical order) Australia, Belgium, Canada, (South) Korea, Norway and Sweden. Borderline countries – those with one strong requisite but not both – are the Netherlands and Switzerland (debt above 200 per cent of GDP and moderate credit of about 5 per cent of GDP per year for the last five years), Finland, France and New Zealand (debt above 175 per cent of GDP and credit of about 5 per cent of GDP), and Malaysia, Singapore and Thailand (debt above 125 per cent of GDP and credit above 10 per cent of GDP).

The only countries that are neither Debt Zombies today nor potential victims in the near future are Austria and Germany amongst the advanced economies, and Argentina, the Czech Republic, Hungary, India, Indonesia, Israel, Mexico, Poland, Saudi Arabia and South Africa amongst the emerging nations. Brazil, Russia and Turkey are borderline

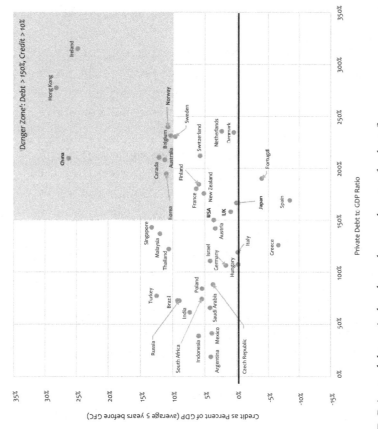

Figure 17. Private debt ratio levels and growth rates for last five years

cases, since while their peak debt ratios are well below the danger zone, their rates of credit growth in recent years have been high, which makes them vulnerable to a deceleration in the rate of growth of private debt.

China alone accounts for 16 per cent of global GDP[8] and 22 per cent of global private debt, so its crisis alone will have a significant impact on the rest of the world. Together, these 17 vulnerable countries account for 28 per cent of global GDP, versus 29 per cent for the USA, and 37 per cent of global private debt, versus 32 per cent for the USA at the time of the GFC. Though the whole group will not experience a crisis at the same time, their transition from debt-driven boom economies to additional members of the Debt Zombies club will slow down growth in these already moribund economies.

The biggest – and the most interesting – of the potential Debt Zombies is of course China. Any criticism of China's current economic situation has to be tempered by an acknowledgement of its extraordinary economic progress over the past thirty years. The abandonment of China's socialist experiment, and the adoption of the 'Capitalist Road' under Deng Xiaoping, transformed China from a country of peasant poverty into a vibrant industrialised economy. I was fortunate to visit China at the very start of its transformation back in 1981/82, and see the Shenzeng Free Trade Zone, where the Zone's management were more than happy to explain their growth strategy.

This relied on exploiting the enormous wage differential between Chinese and Western workers, but this was no different to the strategy of Free Trade Zones in the rest of Asia, where they were already commonplace. What was different about Shenzeng was the requirement that Western companies had to have a Chinese partner, and that 50 per cent of the ownership of the business had to be transferred to the Chinese partner within the first five years. The Chinese were intent on developing a capitalist class and ensuring that knowledge of Western technology was transferred to Chinese businessmen and engineers. I was sceptical of many other aspects of China's attempt to modernise, but confident that this approach was going to work.

And work it did. China grew rapidly as it imported advanced Western technology for its export-oriented factories, as peasants were transformed into industrial workers, and as investment in further expansion was promoted over consumption. The standard of living of the majority of its people has risen dramatically over the last thirty years as a result, and the problems China faces now are those of too much capitalist success, rather than socialist stagnation.

The challenge to China's growth strategy came when the credit engine that had fuelled Western growth died. China's nominal growth rate dropped abruptly, from well over 20 per cent per annum to well under 10 per cent, and a huge exodus of unemployed factory workers began returning to the countryside.

The potential for political turmoil was immense, and in this situation the Chinese government did what Western governments lacked the capacity to do: they instructed their banks – which were largely state-owned in any case – to lend heavily to local property developers. And lend they did: credit grew from 15 per cent of GDP to 40 per cent in just one year (see Figure 18). This huge debt-financed increase in demand, along with an enormous government infrastructure programme, more than made up for the sudden collapse in China's export markets. The biggest credit-driven boom in human history began, and the economy took off as an incredible number of residential apartment blocks went up in Chinese cities. Not only did this policy reverse the domestic labour exodus from the coastal cities, it sucked in so many imports – especially from machinery

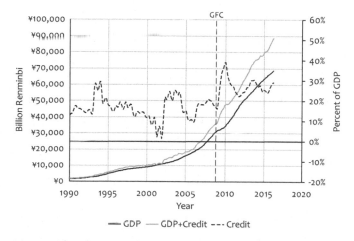

**Figure 18.** China credit and GDP

exporters like South Korea, and resource-rich countries like Australia and Canada – that China's boom significantly attenuated the severity of the Global Financial Crisis for much of the rest of the world.

But this came with an inevitable price: an explosion in China's private debt to GDP ratio, which rose from a relatively low 120 per cent of GDP at the time of the crisis in 2008 to 210 per cent of GDP in March 2016. The effectiveness of the credit stimulus in boosting GDP also plunged rapidly. Nominal GDP growth[9] spurted from 8 per cent p.a. to almost 20 per cent in 2012 as the credit bubble began, but it has since steadily fallen to just 6.5 per cent today.

This bubble has to burst: the growth of debt at this rate and from this level cannot be sustained, even in what is still in large measure a command economy. Many commentators emphasise the peculiar features of China's system to argue that the consequences will be different for China – debt will be written off, state-owned or controlled banks will still be willing to lend and will not be allowed to fail, and so on. But what cannot be avoided is that the credit-driven boost to demand will decline, and this will mean a substantial fall in aggregate demand and income (and capital gains) in China, which can only be countered by a substantial increase in state-financed expenditure.[10]

This is the dilemma for China and indeed for all the Zombies-To-Be: the only way to avoid a substantial decline in aggregate demand (and therefore a recession) *from private sector behaviour alone* is for private debt to continue rising faster than GDP. But in a world in which debt necessitates interest payments, at some point aggregate debt service costs will exceed the income available to meet them.

That same dynamic will play out in those countries which, like China, have become hooked on credit. They face the junkie's dilemma, a choice between going 'Cold Turkey' now, or continuing to shoot up on credit and experience a bigger bust later. China is undoubtedly the biggest country facing the debt junkie's dilemma now. But it doesn't lack for company.

When these countries hit the credit wall, a side-effect of their economic failures will be the end of the careers of their incumbent political leaders.

# 5

# The Political Economy of Private Debt

I've already remarked that Margaret Thatcher was the politician most responsible for 'Labour's Great Recession', as the UK's Tories called the UK's manifestation of the GFC. Though she had long departed from politics by the time the private debt bubble burst, it clearly started on her watch, and thanks to policies she championed. Her 'reforms' were supposed to unleash the creative forces of capitalism, but instead they unleashed the credit-creating capacity of the City of London, and set off a leverage bubble that drove asset prices skyward while starving British industry of development capital.

However, the political opprobrium was worn not by Thatcher, but by the incumbent at the time the debt bubble burst – the Labour Party's Gordon Brown. The government deficit that political spin blamed for the crisis was in fact a consequence of it, and it attenuated the downturn rather than causing it. But this reality was to no avail in the political cycle: Labour lost the 2010 election, and was humiliated in the 2015 campaign when it naively accepted its opponents' spin as fact.

A similar fate is likely to befall the new prime ministers of Canada and Australia, Justin Trudeau and Malcolm Turnbull. Both countries will suffer a serious economic slowdown in the next few years, since the only way they can sustain their current growth rates is for debt to continue growing faster than GDP, as it is doing now: a 3.8 per cent annual growth rate for Canada and 5.7 per cent for Australia, versus nominal GDP growth of zero in Canada and 2 per cent p.a. in Australia. This could happen, especially in Australia where its Central Bank could entice more leveraged property speculation, by dropping official interest rates from their outlier level of 1.5 per cent p.a. to the near zero rate that applies in most of the OECD. But a continuation of this trend is highly unlikely, for two reasons.

Firstly, if the trend continues, then both countries will have private debt to GDP ratios that exceed 250 per cent by 2020. This would be the highest level ever recorded in major OECD economies, and smaller only than tiny Luxembourg and the peculiar vassal state of Hong Kong.

Secondly, the corporate sectors of both countries are likely to reduce their debt levels strongly in the next few years, since the China-motivated minerals boom in both countries is now over. This corporate sector deleveraging will counteract any rise in household leverage, so that the required increase in household leverage to sustain their bubbles becomes simply unthinkable. For example, if the corporate debt ratio merely stabilised, then Canadian household debt would need to rise from 96 per cent to 143 per cent of GDP by 2020 to compensate. Australia, which already has the highest household debt ratio in the world of 125 per cent of GDP, would need to reach 170 per cent. That simply isn't going to happen.

Consequently, both countries are very likely to suffer a severe economic crisis before 2020 – and possibly as early as 2017. This crisis will be blamed on the incumbents and the economic policies they follow – and in Canada's case, it will mean that Trudeau's decision to run a government deficit, which he flagged during the electoral campaign, will be blamed for the crisis.

Far from being the cause of the crisis, Trudeau's deficit will in fact soften the blow of collapsing credit, when it comes (while Turnbull's swing towards austerity will make Australia's crisis worse). But the peculiar dynamics of debt mean that casual observation supports the proposition that a politician who either triggers or benefits from a debt bubble is a good economic manager – capable of delivering good times and also running a government surplus – while the politician who wears the aftermath of the bubble stands accused of being an economic incompetent who presides over a serious recession and runs a government deficit.

This is why America's ex-President Bill Clinton (Democrat), at one political extreme, and Australia's ex-Prime Minister John Howard (from Australia's conservative Liberal Party), at the other, are both falsely feted as good economic managers. In fact, both leaders happened to come into power when a previous private debt-induced downturn had come to a close and a new debt bubble had begun, firing up the economy's performance with credit and filling government coffers with tax revenue.

In Clinton's case, he took the political reins of the country just as the business sector had ceased deleveraging after the Savings and Loans crisis. Business debt, which largely financed investment (especially in telecommunications), started growing at the same speed as GDP, while household debt began to rise. The combined effect was to generate credit-fuelled demand and debt-financed investment that gave America its last major technological boost, with the expansion of telecommunications and the parallel development of the Internet. The actual technology was truly transformative. But it and the credit that enabled it led to a speculative euphoria, as firstly telecommunications firms and then DotCom companies were endowed with sky-high market valuations. This bubble had to burst, and did so shortly after the archetypal DotCom market index, the Nasdaq, peaked in March 2000.

When it did, business borrowing plunged once more, from over 6 per cent of GDP to under 1 per cent. But shortly after the plunge in business borrowing began, borrowing by the household sector accelerated dramatically, from 5 per cent of GDP per year in 2000 to almost 10 per cent of GDP per year on average between 2003 and 2006.

As a consequence, the growth of private debt barely skipped a beat across the DotCom Crash of 2000. Whereas aggregate credit fell to just above 2 per cent of GDP during the 1990s recession, it didn't fall below 7 per cent of GDP during the 2001 recession. From that very high low, it raced to 15 per cent of GDP at the height of the subprime boom, as lending to households dramatically overtook lending to businesses as the main profit centre for banks. Household debt, which had been roughly the same scale as corporate debt since the 1950s, grew to 1.4 times corporate debt in 2005. Lending for speculation on real estate became the main function of the private banking sector.

Clinton was long gone from office when the negative consequences of this speculative bubble were felt, and he – and Hillary today – can without irony trumpet his superior skills as an economic manager over Bush Junior, on whose watch the fatal flaws in a credit bubble finally came home to roost. But Bush was no more responsible for the crisis, when it came, than was Brown in the UK. He merely had the misfortune to be the incumbent when the house of credit cards collapsed.

Debt thus plays a pernicious role in our political system, as well as in our economy. Because a private debt bubble stimulates demand while it is expanding, the incumbent on whose watch the bubble begins gets an undeserved reputation for effective economic management. Then when the bust occurs, the blowout in government spending that results lands the hapless incumbent at the time with the charge of being a poor steward of the nation's finances. The political system rewards the lackey of credit who triggers the unsustainable boom, and makes a political victim of the incumbent when the boom collapses.

But the public would not make this misidentification without the help of the misinformation spread by the economics profession. Mainstream economists are the real culprits in the crisis and its aftermath, since they advise governments that credit is in fact benign, that rising private debt is no cause for alarm, that a bigger and politically more dominant finance sector is in fact good for the economy, and that the government should avoid running deficits.[1] Their views were devoid of any real appreciation of the role of credit in a capitalist system – and of the government's role as a money creator in a mixed market–state economy – but because they were endowed with the mantle of economic expertise, they were listened to, while economic heretics like Minsky, Goodwin, Godley and myself were ignored.

The mainstream's ignorant advice also supports the public's naive perception of the economic data, which the UK Tories exploited so well to blame the 2008 crisis on the government deficit. A simple look at the data confirms that government surpluses coincide with good times and government deficits coincide with bad times – so deficits must be responsible for the crisis, mustn't they?

In reality, these views are as misguided as the observation that the Sun rises in the East and sets in the West every day, so that therefore the Sun must rotate around the Earth. Only crackpots believe this today, but half a millennium ago it was both the common belief and the belief of the 'experts' on the Heavens, the Ptolemaic astronomers.

Today, informed by the Copernican vision of the universe, an ordinary member of the public can talk of 'sunrise' and 'sunset' while still knowing that the Earth orbits the Sun, and not vice versa. But it took the development and promulgation of the Newtonian model before that became the rule. However, in economics, when the public turns to the accepted economic experts for guidance, they hear arguments that reinforce a naive perception of the data.

Mainstream economists have argued relentlessly – at least until the crisis in 2008 – for deregulation of the finance sector, and they have developed economic theories (such as the 'Modigliani–Miller Theorem') which have effectively championed the growth of debt finance. Forty years of Neoliberalism – which is effectively introductory Neoclassical economics disguised as a political philosophy – have transformed the global economy so that on paper it looks much like the model world of a first-year economics textbook. Finance markets have been deregulated, unions have been destroyed, tariffs have been dropped worldwide, competition policy is applied to basic services like health, education and transport.

This is a world that was supposed to function like clockwork. Instead, it performed poorly (compared to the more regulated 1950s and 1960s), and its clock stopped ticking when the Global Financial Crisis hit, because this model world of Neoclassical fantasy omitted key elements of the real world that unfortunately cannot be expunged from the real world itself. Credit matters here; the real world is always in disequilibrium, and many of the so-called 'imperfections' removed by Neoliberal reformers removed feedback effects that attenuated capitalism's inherent instability.

After the crisis, even proponents of Neoliberalism like the IMF are starting to abandon it (Ostry et al., 2016). But the damage they have done has not been undone. Thanks to their mismanagement, the global economy has been saddled with a level of private debt that, on the statistics gathered here, is not only unprecedented since the end of the Second World War, but also unprecedented in the history of capitalism. That is evident in Figure 16, which tracks UK debt since 1880; it is also apparent in the long-term debt data for the USA going back to 1834 (see Figure 19).[2]

The UK and USA have a much higher level

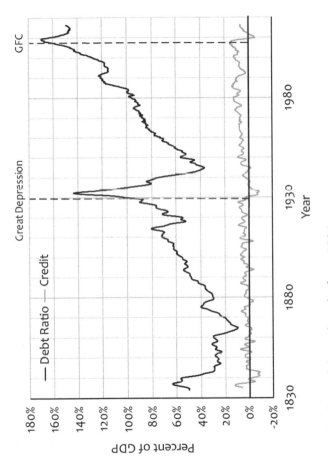

Figure 19. US private debt and credit from 1834

113

of private debt in the post-war period than ever before, and this arguably undermines part of the case that progressives – and indeed Minsky – make for 'Big Government'. Minsky argued that 'Big Government' was one way to stabilise an unstable economy, but the historical record implies that Big Government has in the end led to the private sector taking on even more leverage than it would do without the stabilising impact of a rise in government spending during a downturn. Minsky's famous observation that 'stability is destabilising' applies to government policy as well: an extended period of economic tranquillity – which is what Big Government gave capitalism after the Second World War – has encouraged a lax attitude towards the dangers of excessive private sector debt and a bloated and too powerful financial system.

Our escape from this trap will not be easy, not just because reversing the mistakes of the past is difficult, but because the hold that conventional economic wisdom has on what is regarded as politically acceptable economic policy is just too strong. Since the crisis is fundamentally due to excessive private debt, we need to do whatever is necessary to reduce that level of private debt, without in the process crushing the economy under the weight of negative credit. But we won't do it – or at least we won't do it deliberately.

# 6

# A Cynic's Conclusion

Market-driven mechanisms alone are unlikely to reduce the debt to GDP ratio, for the reason that Irving Fisher identified during the Great Depression: 'Fisher's Paradox' that, in a deleveraging and deflationary environment, *'The more the debtors pay, the more they owe'* (Fisher, 1933, p. 344, emphasis added). Just as net debt creation creates money and adds to demand, net debt repayment destroys money and subtracts from demand. Especially in a low-inflation environment, this reduces economic activity: nominal GDP falls, and net capital gains on asset sales become negative. The result is that the debt to GDP ratio falls only slightly, if at all, for a large reduction in nominal debt, because nominal GDP falls at the same time.

Japan's post-1990 experience also implies that private sector debt won't be reduced sufficiently by government sector spending alone. Japanese government debt has risen from 150 per cent to 220 per cent of GDP since 2008, yet private debt has remained static at about 165 per cent of GDP across that period. Japan has avoided a depression thanks to government spending, as Richard Koo (2009) argues, but it still has not escaped the private debt trap it first succumbed to a quarter of a century ago.

The scale of government spending needed to bring down private debt appears to be accepted only during crises like the Second World War. Money is, ultimately, our fragile means to mobilise existing resources and enable the creation of new ones, and when an existential threat arises, we forget money's frailty and mobilise and create those resources directly: no one in Britain in 1940 evoked 'Sound Finance' as a reason not to build weapons, when the alternative was a German invasion. UK government debt rose by 44 per cent of GDP in that one year, and from 220 per cent to 340 per cent of GDP over the course of the War. This indirectly enabled private sector debt to fall from 70 per cent of GDP to 30 per cent, thanks to the huge increase in public spending – and the rise in nominal GDP.

Without such an existential threat, government deficits are likely to be like those run in Japan: too small, and too quickly withdrawn when the economy shows signs of revival while private debt levels are still too high. This is especially so since private debt levels today are so much higher than they were at the start of the Second World War (the UK's private debt level today is 160 per cent of GDP, versus 70 per cent just before the outbreak of the War).

If neither market nor indirect government action is likely to reduce private debt sufficiently, the only options are either a direct reduction of private debt, or an increase in the money supply that indirectly reduces the debt burden. Among the handful of researchers to have correctly identified private debt as the key problem afflicting the global economy today (Bezemer, 2011a; Hudson, 2009; Keen, 2014; King, 2016; Mian & Sufi, 2015; Schularick & Taylor, 2012; Turner, 2016; Wolf, 2014; see also Bezemer, 2010), Mian and Sufi (2015, ch. 10) have advocated direct debt forgiveness, while Wolf (2014), Turner (2016) and King (2016) have proposed what is colloquially described as 'helicopter money' – the use of the Central Bank's capacity to create money to inject money directly into personal bank accounts.

Both proposals on their own face legitimate objections. Debt forgiveness appears to favour debtors over savers – and negative reactions to this prospect during 2009 played a large role in the rise of the Tea Party in the USA (Mian & Sufi, 2015, ch. 10). 'Helicopter money' doesn't have this drawback, but it doesn't necessarily reduce the level of private debt either: it simply dilutes the effect of outstanding debt by increasing the money supply. The scale of the injection that would be needed to bring private debt back to a level where a credit slowdown doesn't cause a crisis – something well under 100 per cent of GDP – is also enormous.

I suggest a melding of the two approaches, in what I have called a 'Modern Debt Jubilee':[1] make a direct injection of money into all private bank accounts, but require that its first use is to pay down debt. Debt would thus be directly reduced as with Mian and Sufi's proposal, but debtors would not be rewarded relative to savers.

This proposal is clearly more easily stated than implemented. Household debt is more easily targeted than corporate debt; many debt contracts have covenants designed to make early repayment difficult if not impossible; and securitisation of debt creates enormous legal minefields. But it is also a more flexible method than Mian and Sufi's necessarily legalistic remedy, and it could be trialled on a much smaller scale than would be necessary with a pure helicopter money approach.

On its own, a Modern Debt Jubilee would not be enough: all it would do is reset the clock to allow another speculative debt bubble to take off. Currently, private money creation is 'a by-product of the activities of a casino' (Keynes, 1936, p. 159), rather than what it primarily should be: the consequence of the funding of corporate investment and entrepreneurial activity (Schumpeter, 1934, p. 74). We have to stop bank lending causing asset bubbles, while making it profitable for banks to lend to companies and entrepreneurs.

One supreme weakness of our current system is that it actually encourages the public to want higher leverage: if two people with equivalent incomes compete to buy a house right now, the winner is the one who gets the bigger bank loan. This could be prevented by limiting bank lending to some multiple of the income-earning capacity of the asset being purchased – say ten times its annual rental income (actual or imputed). With this rule in place (which I call the 'PILL', for 'Property Income-Limited Leverage'), the maximum loan to buy a given property would be the same for all would-be buyers, and the incentive for buyers of equivalent incomes would be to save a larger deposit, not take out a larger loan.

But this reform alone would leave banks with no profitable business model, and the rate of growth of the money supply would plummet – especially since politicians and the public are still enthralled with the myth of 'Sound Finance' that asserts that a government should 'live within its means' and spend no more than it raises in taxes. In fact, as 'Modern Monetary Theory' (MMT) proponents rightly assert (Wray, 2003), the government is the sole institution in society that is not revenue-constrained, because it is the only institution in society that 'owns its own bank', the Central Bank. Government spending can be financed by Central Bank purchases of Treasury bonds, and to the extent that this happens, money is created, and government spending can systematically exceed taxation without imposing a burden on current or future generations.

Whatever you might think of how well the government spends money, when it spends more than it gets back in taxation, this boosts the amount of money in circulation, and that finances private sector activity. The belief that governments should be balanced in the long run is in fact a belief that governments should abdicate the role of money creation solely to private banks – and we've all seen what a great job they've done with that responsibility in the last few decades.

Lobby groups that are aware of this, such as Positive Money in the UK and the American

Monetary Institute in the USA, argue for ending the ability of private banks to create money, and vesting that right solely in the government (or an independent statutory authority).[2] Banks would still have a role in this system, but they would profit only by arbitraging the difference between loan rates and deposit rates when they lent out money deposited in investment accounts (rather than savings accounts), or between loan rates and the reserve rate if they borrowed directly from the Central Bank.

I am sympathetic with the sentiment of these proposals, but I believe they go too far: arbitrage profits alone won't entice bank lending to entrepreneurs, who would be as stifled of funds in this proposed system as they are in our current one.

At present, banks have a very legitimate reason not to fund entrepreneurs. If they do fund them, perhaps four out of five will go bankrupt, while the bank would only earn interest income off the one that survives. It's not a successful business model for debt – but it is a successful business model for venture capital firms. However, venture capital investment in entrepreneurs doesn't create money, whereas bank lending does.

We could meld the two by allowing 'Entrepreneurial Equity Loans' that would enable a bank to take an equity position rather than to issue a loan: the issuing of an 'EEL' would create money for an entrepreneur, and give the bank an equity stake in the venture it financed. Four out of five entrepreneurs would still fail, but the bank would make a capital gain on the one that succeeded, as well as earning dividends.

We also need to accept that capitalism would have financial crises even if all lending were entirely responsible. As Minsky argued (and my simple macroeconomic models demonstrate), crises can still occur even if all investment is for productive purposes, since the financial system is 'capable of both generating signals that induce an accelerating desire to invest and of financing that accelerating investment' (Minsky, 1969, p. 224). Booms and bust are in the nature of capitalism. So we can expect the trend for a rising private debt to GDP ratio, like that in US private debt from 1945 on, to continue even in a reformed financial system.

The only way to counter this is to make the private debt to GDP ratio as significant an entity in economic management as the inflation and unemployment rates are today, and to employ the State's capacity to create money as a tool of macroeconomic management specifically to reduce private debt when it starts to rise to a dangerous level – which is well under 100 per cent of GDP, and far below the levels that unbridled finance has saddled us with today.

These reforms to banking and macroeconomic management would I believe create a better banking system, and a more stable but still vibrant capitalist economy. But I also believe that these reforms, or anything like them, have next to no chance of ever being implemented. So what to do?

The first thing we have no choice but to do is to wear the consequences of the current trends in debt and credit. The nine to seventeen countries I've identified as Debt-Zombies-To-Be will suffer credit crunches in the next few years, and then join the nine countries who are already Debt Zombies after their own crises in 1990 (Japan) and 2008 (the USA, Denmark, Ireland, the Netherlands, New Zealand, Portugal, Spain and the UK). When that happens, the majority of the world's economies will be in the doldrums due to excessive private debt, and the world will experience the kind of economic malaise that has afflicted Japan for over a quarter of a century.

We could escape this trap with only moderate difficulty, using the policies outlined in this chapter. But these are unlikely even to be discussed in the portals of power, let alone implemented, because today's power brokers are still in thrall to the delusional vision of the economy promulgated by mainstream economists.

Policies and reforms like those suggested above rely upon persuading politicians that mainstream economics advice can't be trusted, and that it's worth risking unconventional policies instead. Even if that could be done, large swathes of the public would oppose those policies because of a mindset about both economics and public morality which has been shaped by that same unrealistic view of the economy. The public treats bank debt as morally equivalent to debts between individuals, where failure to repay forces a genuine loss on the lender. This misidentification is aided and abetted by the mainstream model of banks, which ignores their role as 'money factories' which can and do periodically create too much debt, and instead pretends that they are 'money warehouses' that only lend out what the public deposits with them.

As long as that model holds sway over politicians and the general public, sensible reforms will face an uphill battle – even without the resistance of the finance sector to the proposals, which of course will be enormous. There has been more progress in getting mainstream economists to concede that their worldview is wrong than I had expected to see when I began my public campaign to reform economics more than a decade ago (Blanchard, 2016; Kocherlakota, 2016; Romer, 2016). But it could take a decade before these proposals might be even tentatively applied, and I doubt that the fractious societies of Europe and America could cope with another ten years of economic stagnation.

This policy paralysis has led many private citizens to contemplate whether it is possible to undertake commerce without needing State or bank money – often in response to being burnt themselves in the 2008 crash, when credit dried up and banks called in loans without warning. Without the handicap of a false economic theory to unlearn, they have come to understand money much better than do the official custodians of our money supply in Central Banks (with the honourable exception of the Bank of England: see McLeay et al., 2014). In particular, some entrepreneurs have taken on board Minsky's observation that 'in principle every unit can "create" money – the only problem being to get it "accepted"' (1986, p. 86), and have created a range of parallel currencies.

Lacking the status of a government as a fiat currency issuer, or a banking licence to legitimise their currencies in the eyes of potential users, these would-be non-bank private money providers need something other than the capacity to levy taxes in their currency, or the trust that comes from being a registered bank. The alternatives are valuable commodities used as a currency, barter of goods at market value using a parallel currency, or an encryption and data storage system that provides equivalent security and storage capabilities to a registered bank.

The first can be dismissed immediately: despite the ridiculous number of 'gold bugs' in the world who believe the myth that, in the past, gold was money (Graeber, 2011), there is not enough of any valuable commodities – let alone gold – to enable them to be used as money, and I know of no parallel currency system based on them.

Barter-based systems, on the other hand, have existed since at least 1991, when Bartercard Australia was established.[3] It now has operations in eight countries and turns over about US$600 million a year, largely at the tradesman and small business end of the commercial spectrum, with a basic unit of exchange valued at 1 local currency unit wherever it operates. One of the latest systems, IEX Global,[4] is designed to enable high net worth individuals and large corporations to transact securely without money. It requires participants to tender for sale assets or services with a minimum independently assessed value of US$1 million (or the near equivalent in domestic currency), and issues tradeable 'VBonds' that can be used to buy any asset or product listed for sale on the IEX exchange.

Bitcoin is the most well-known virtual currency, the essential idea of which is to transcend the current 'triangular' monetary system – in which payment necessarily involves a buyer, a seller and a third party (a bank) that records the transaction (Graziani, 1989, p. 3)[5] – with a two-sided system where a computer protocol records the transaction, and makes forgery of transactions and theft of accumulated currency units impossible. However, this computer protocol is necessarily expensive to run in terms of both computer time and power consumption, and very slow. The value of Bitcoin is also too unstable to function as a substitute for everyday money. The 'blockchain' technology, whose difficulty of computing provides virtual currencies with their alternative to the fraud prevention facilities of banks, may yet revolutionise business record keeping, but the virtual currencies themselves have some substantial way to go to provide a viable alternative to bank money.

I don't believe that any of these systems can scale to the level that they make up for the failures of our private-bank-based monetary system – let alone that they could ever replace banks completely. But while the world suffers from a credit crunch caused by both the inherent nature of debt-based money, and the inept handling of it by the mainstream economists, some alternatives that enable more economic activity are needed. These parallel currency systems will be ready to take advantage of the next economic crisis, and will provide some relief to its victims who find themselves with unmoveable merchandise or assets as a result. If any of them succeed on a large scale, that practical experience could, in the end, do more to force reform of the banking system than any amount of intellectual argument.

So, to answer the question this book poses, no, we cannot avoid financial crises in the Debt-Zombies-To-Be, because the economic prerequisites of excessive private debt and excessive reliance on credit have already been set. Nor can we avoid stagnation in the Walking Dead of Debt, so long as we ignore the private debt overhang that is its primary cause.

We could dramatically lessen the impact of these crises if political leaders and their economic advisers understood how they are caused by credit bubbles, and we could escape stagnation if they were willing to use the State's money-creating capacity to reduce the post-crisis overhang of excessive private debt. But because they are not, crises in the Debt-Zombies-To-Be are inevitable between now and 2020, and the plunge in their credit-based demand will take what little wind remains out of the sails of global commerce. Stagnation at the global level will be the outcome, not because of an absence of new ideas from scientists and engineers, as 'secular stagnation' devotees assert, but because mainstream economists have clung to delusional ideas about the nature of capitalism, even as the real world, time and time again, has proven them wrong.

# Notes

### *Acknowledgements*

1 See www.bis.org/statistics/totcredit.htm and www.bis.org/statistics/pp.htm (source: National Sources, BIS Residential Property Price database).
2 See www.bis.org/publ/arpdf/ar2007e.htm.


### *Chapter 1  From Triumph to Crisis in Economics*

1 This collection of relatively short papers is by far the best introduction to Minsky's work.


### *Chapter 2  Microeconomics, Macroeconomics and Complexity*

1 The only limitation was that the shape had to be fitted by a polynomial – the sum of powers of x, $x^2$, $x^3$, and so on: 'every polynomial . . . is an excess demand function for a specified commodity in some $n$ commodity economy' (Sonnenschein, 1972).

# Notes

2 I'm sure some mainstream macroeconomists will dispute the use of this third definition, but I cover why it is essential in Chapter 4, 'The Smoking Gun of Credit'. See also Kumhof and Jakab (2015), which shows the dramatic impact of introducing private debt and endogenous money into a mainstream DSGE model.

3 This compares to seven variables, forty-nine parameters, and also random (stochastic) terms in the Smets-Wouters DSGE model mentioned earlier (see Romer, 2016, p. 12). See www.profstevekeen.com/crisis/models for the model's equations and derivation. For the mathematical properties of this class of models, see Grasselli and Costa Lima (2012).

4 Notably its linear behavioural rules and the absence of price dynamics means that the cycles are symmetrical – booms are as big as busts. These deficiencies are addressed in the model that generates Figure 5. There are issues also with these definitions, notably that of capital, which should not be ignored as they were after the 'Cambridge Controversies' (Sraffa, 1960; Samuelson 1956). But these can be addressed by a disaggregation process, and are also made easier by acknowledging the role of energy in production. These topics are beyond the scope of this book, but I will address them in future more technical publications.

5 'The source of financing most correlated with investment is long-term debt ... debt plays a key role in accommodating year-by-year variation in investment.'

6 The wages share of output was a proxy for inflation in this simple model without price dynamics. The more complete model shown in Figure 5 explicitly includes inflation, and shows the same trend for inflation as found in the data.

## Chapter 3 The Lull and the Storm

1 Bezemer (2009) notes twelve other economists (including me) who both warned of the crisis and had an explanation of it that went beyond worrying about the US housing bubble.

2 Paul Ormerod, Rickard Nyman and I have recently done an empirical test of causality which found that accelerating mortgage debt 'Granger-causes' house price changes, whereas the reverse is not true.

## Chapter 4 The Smoking Gun of Credit

1 'The monetary data for the United States are quite remarkable, and tend to underscore the stinging critique of the Fed's policy choices by Friedman and Schwartz ... The proximate cause of this decline in M1 was continued contraction in the ratio of base to reserves, which reinforced rather than offset declines in the money multiplier. This tightening ... locates much of the blame for the early (pre-1931) slow-down in world monetary aggregates with the Federal Reserve.'

2 'And although there are a lot of Americans who understandably think that government money would

be better spent going directly to families and businesses instead of banks – "where's our bailout?", they ask – the truth is that a dollar of capital in a bank can actually result in eight or ten dollars of loans to families and businesses, a multiplier effect that can ultimately lead to a faster pace of economic growth.'

3 The same observation can be made for the prices of all other commodities. But the issue here is that you are using money as your 'measuring stick', and you can only affect all prices and incomes equally by doubling them in money terms *if money itself is costless* – if it is simply a token that in itself doesn't generate incomes or costs – and if people hold only trivial amounts of it, and don't trade it *per se* between each other for a money price. This would be the case if and only if money was both 'pure fiat' – a token issued by some non-market entity (like the government) – and it wasn't stored, or lent between agents in return for interest payments. None of these assumptions is true: money is part fiat money (created by the government) and part credit money (created by banks); and money is stored, and lent at interest between agents.

4 For the full technical argument, see www.profsteve keen.com/crisis/demand.

5 There is a real cause of a potential slowdown in economic growth today that was not relevant when Hansen wrote: the decline in energy output per unit of energy input (known as 'Energy Return On Energy Invested' or EROEI) due to declining availability of oil, and the transition from fossil fuels to renewable energy (see https://en.wikipedia.org/

wiki/Energy_returned_on_energy_invested). But this is not part of Summers' thinking, since Neoclassical economics does not acknowledge any role for energy in production – and nor does any other approach to economics as yet. A discussion of this topic is beyond the scope of this book, but see www.forbes.com/sites/stevekeen/2016/08/19/incorporating-energy-into-production-functions.

6 The other countries identified as current Debt Zombies are profiled in the website for this book, www.profstevekeen.com/crisis.

7 Ireland's position may be a side-effect of its tax system and GDP accounting methodology (see www.irishtimes.com/business/economy/do-not-be-fooled-by-bizarre-fiction-of-cso-growth-figures-1.2719555). Hong Kong's data is very peculiar: household debt is less than a third of corporate debt, which at over 210 per cent of GDP is higher than the total private non-financial-sector debt of most countries. Hong Kong's political circumstances and entrepôt status may mean that this debt is booked to corporations domiciled there, but the financing burden may not actually be borne by the Hong Kong economy.

8 Where 'global' means the combined GDPs (in US$ terms) of the forty-one countries in the BIS database.

9 I trust China's nominal data more than its 'real' since the latter is so easily manipulated with price indices.

10 There is one further potential 'out' for China: the fact that its 'private' banks are partly state-owned

and largely state-directed means that they can function as an extension of the Central Bank, and ignore the failure of debtors to repay debt – thus effectively turning credit money into fiat money. This may lie behind anecdotal evidence that Chinese banks are financing infrastructure programmes throughout the developing world – and thus providing export sales for Chinese corporations and work for Chinese workers who would otherwise be unemployed.

## Chapter 5 The Political Economy of Private Debt

1 The core message here is 'Ricardian Equivalence', which asserts that government deficits now must be offset by surpluses later, and that knowing this, individuals today respond to a government deficit by putting aside money to pay future taxes – so that the intended stimulatory effect of a government deficit is perfectly offset by reduced private sector spending (Barro, 1996). When critics pointed out to Barro that this argument was easily undermined by the observation that these offsetting taxes might not be levied until after today's taxpayers had died, he responded with the bizarre proposition that 'a network of intergenerational transfers makes the typical person a part of an extended family that goes on indefinitely. In this setting, households capitalize the entire array of expected future taxes, and thereby plan effectively with an infinite horizon' (Barro, 1989, p. 40). Less delusional mainstream economists

like Paul Krugman and Michael Woodford argue for government deficits during recessions, but Barro's extremism is the starting position for the mainstream as a whole.

2 This chart amalgamates Federal Reserve data from 1945 with two Census series on private debt and bank lending dating back to 1834. The Census data has been normalised to Federal Reserve levels, using substantial overlaps between the series to ensure that this practice was justified.

### *Chapter 6  A Cynic's Conclusion*

1 See www.debtdeflation.com/blogs/manifesto.
2 See http://positivemoney.org and www.monetary.org.
3 See www.bartercard.com.au.
4 See www.iex.global. I am a consultant to IEX.
5 Cash transactions still notionally involve a third party – the government whose Central Bank issues the notes.

# Bibliography

Anderson, P. W. (1972) More is Different. *Science*, 177, 393–6.

Barro, R. J. (1989) The Ricardian Approach to Budget Deficits. *Journal of Economic Perspectives*, 3, 37–54.

Barro, R. (1996) Ricardo and Budget Deficits. In: Capie, F. & Wood, G. E. (eds), *Monetary Economics in the 1990s: The Henry Thornton Lectures, numbers 9–17*, New York: St. Martin's Press.

Bernanke, B. S. (2000) *Essays on the Great Depression*, Princeton: Princeton University Press.

Bernanke, B. S. (2004) Panel Discussion: What Have We Learned Since October 1979? Conference on Reflections on Monetary Policy 25 Years after October 1979, St. Louis, Missouri: Federal Reserve Bank of St. Louis.

Bezemer, D. J. (2009) 'No One Saw This Coming': *Understanding Financial Crisis Through Accounting*

*Models*, Groningen, the Netherlands: Faculty of Economics, University of Groningen.

Bezemer, D. J. (2010) Understanding Financial Crisis Through Accounting Models. *Accounting, Organizations and Society*, 35, 676–88.

Bezemer, D. J. (2011a) Causes of Financial Instability: Don't Forget Finance. Levy Economics Institute, Economics Working Paper Archive.

Bezemer, D. J. (2011b) The Credit Crisis and Recession as a Paradigm Test. *Journal of Economic Issues*, 45, 1–18.

Blanchard, O. (2016) *Do DSGE Models Have a Future?* Peterson Institute for International Economics. At: https://piie.com/publications/policy-briefs/do-dsge-models-have-future.

Blanchard, O., Dell'Ariccia, G. & Mauro, P. (2010) Rethinking Macroeconomic Policy. *Journal of Money, Credit, and Banking*, 42, 199–215.

Blatt, J. M. (1983) *Dynamic Economic Systems: A Post-Keynesian Approach*, Armonk, NY: M.E. Sharpe.

Cole, H. L. & Ohanian, L. E. (2004) New Deal Policies and the Persistence of the Great Depression: A General Equilibrium Analysis. *Journal of Political Economy*, 112, 779–816.

Conservative Party (2015) The Conservative Party Manifesto 2015. At: https://www.conservatives.com/manifesto.

Copeland, M. A. (1951) *A Study of Moneyflows in the United States*, New York: NBER.

# Bibliography

Cotis, J.-P. (2007) Editorial: Achieving Further Rebalancing. In: OECD (ed.), *OECD Economic Outlook*, Paris: OECD.

Eggertsson, G. B. & Krugman, P. (2012) Debt, Deleveraging, and the Liquidity Trap: A Fisher-Minsky-Koo approach. *Quarterly Journal of Economics*, 127, 1469–1513.

Fama, E. F. & French, K. R. (1999a) The Corporate Cost of Capital and the Return on Corporate Investment. *Journal of Finance*, 54, 1939–67.

Fama, E. F. & French, K. R. (1999b) Dividends, Debt, Investment, and Earnings. Working Papers, University of Chicago.

Fama, E. F. & French, K. R. (2002) Testing Trade-Off and Pecking Order Predictions about Dividends and Debt. *Review of Financial Studies*, 15, 1–33.

Fisher, I. (1933) The Debt-Deflation Theory of Great Depressions. *Econometrica*, 1, 337–57.

FOMC (2007) FOMC Transcript. New York: Federal Reserve Open Monetary Committee.

Godley, W. (2001) The Developing Recession in the United States. *Banca Nazionale del Lavoro Quarterly Review*, 54, 417–25.

Godley, W. & Izurieta, A. (2002) The Case for a Severe Recession. *Challenge*, 45, 27–51.

Godley, W. & Izurieta, A. (2004) The US Economy: Weaknesses of the 'Strong' Recovery. *Banca Nazionale del Lavoro Quarterly Review*, 57, 131–9.

# Bibliography

Godley, W., Izurieta, A., Gray, H. P. & Dilyard, J. R. (2005) Strategic Prospects and Policies for the US Economy. In: Gray, H. P. & Dilyard, J. R. (eds), *Globalization and Economic and Financial Instability*, Cheltenham: Elgar.

Godley, W. & McCarthy, G. (1998) Fiscal Policy Will Matter. *Challenge*, 41, 38–54.

Godley, W. & Wray, L. R. (2000) Is Goldilocks Doomed? *Journal of Economic Issues*, 34, 201–6.

Goldenfeld, N. & Kadanoff, L. P. (1999) Simple Lessons from Complexity. *Science*, 284, 87–9.

Goodwin, R. M. (1967) A Growth Cycle. In: Feinstein, C. H. (ed.), *Socialism, Capitalism and Economic Growth*, Cambridge: Cambridge University Press.

Gorman, W. M. (1953) Community Preference Fields. *Econometrica*, 21, 63–80.

Graeber, D. (2011) *Debt: The First 5,000 Years*, New York: Melville House.

Grasselli, M. & Costa Lima, B. (2012) An Analysis of the Keen Model for Credit Expansion, Asset Price Bubbles and Financial Fragility. *Mathematics and Financial Economics*, 6, 191–210.

Grattan, M. (2010) Treasury's Unleashed Rock Star. *Sydney Morning Herald*, Sydney, Fairfax, 14 May.

Graziani, A. (1989) The Theory of the Monetary Circuit. *Thames Papers in Political Economy*, Spring, 1–26.

# Bibliography

Greenspan, A. (2005) Testimony of Chairman Alan Greenspan: The Economic Outlook. Washington, DC: Joint Economic Committee, US Congress.

Hansen, A. H. (1934) Capital Goods and the Restoration of Purchasing Power. *Proceedings of the Academy of Political Science*, 16, 11–19.

Hansen, A. (1939) Economic Progress and Declining Population Growth. *American Economic Review*, 29, 1–15.

Hicks, J. R. (1937) Mr. Keynes and the 'Classics': A Suggested Interpretation. *Econometrica*, 5, 147–59.

Hicks, J. (1981) IS-LM: An Explanation. *Journal of Post Keynesian Economics*, 3, 139–54.

Hills, S., Thomas, R. & Dimsdale, N. (2010) The UK Recession in Context – What Do Three Centuries of Data Tell Us? *Bank of England Quarterly Bulletin*, Q4, 277–91.

Hudson, M. (2009) Why the 'Miracle of Compound Interest' Leads to Financial Crises. *Ensayos de Economia*, 19, 15–33.

Keen, S. (1995a) Comment on Feldman's Structural Model of Economic Growth. In: Groenewegen, P. & McFarlane, B. (eds), *Socialist Thought in the Post Cold War Era*, Manila: Journal of Contemporary Asia Publishers.

Keen, S. (1995b) Finance and Economic Breakdown: Modeling Minsky's 'Financial Instability Hypothesis'. *Journal of Post Keynesian Economics*, 17, 607–35.

# Bibliography

Keen, S. (2005) Expert Opinion, *Permanent Mortgages vs Cooks*, Sydney: Legal Aid NSW.

Keen, S. (2007) Debtwatch May 2007: Booming on Borrowed Money. At: http://www.debtdeflation.com/blogs/2007/04/30/debtwatch-may-2005-booming-on-borrowed-money.

Keen, S. (2011) *Debunking Economics: The Naked Emperor Dethroned?*, London: Zed Books.

Keen, S. (2014) Secular Stagnation and Endogenous Money. *Real World Economics Review*, 66, 2–11.

Keynes, J. M. (1936) *The General Theory of Employment, Interest and Money*, London: Macmillan.

Keynes, J. M. (1937) The General Theory of Employment. *Quarterly Journal of Economics*, 51, 209–23.

Kindleberger, C. P. (1978) *Manias, Panics, and Crashes*, New York: Basic Books.

King, M. (2016) *The End of Alchemy*, London: Little Brown.

Kirman, A. (1989) The Intrinsic Limits of Modern Economic Theory: The Emperor Has No Clothes. *Economic Journal*, 99, 126–39.

Kocherlakota, N. (2016) Toy Models. At: https://docs.google.com/viewer?a=v&pid=sites&srcid=ZGVmYXVsdGRvbWFpbnxrb2NoZXJsYWtvdGEwMDl8Z3g6MTAyZmIzODcxNGZiOGY4Yg.

Koo, R. (2009) *The Holy Grail of Macroeconomics: Lessons from Japan's Great Recession*, Singapore: Wiley.

# Bibliography

Kornai, J. (1979) Resource-Constrained versus Demand-Constrained Systems. *Econometrica*, 47, 801–19.

Krugman, P. (2012a) *End this Depression Now!*, New York: W. W. Norton.

Krugman, P. (2012b) Oh My, Steve Keen Edition. *The Conscience of a Liberal*. At: http://krugman.blogs. nytimes.com/2012/04/02/oh-my-steve-keen-edition.

Krugman, P. (2012c) Banking Mysticism. *The Conscience of a Liberal*. At: http://krugman.blogs.nytimes. com/2012/03/27/banking-mysticism.

Krugman, P. (2013) Abenomics and Interest Rates: A Finger Exercise (Wonkish). *The Conscience of a Liberal*. At: http://krugman.blogs.nytimes.com/2013/06/10/aben omics-and-interest-rates-a-finger-exercise-wonkish.

Kumhof, M. & Jakab, Z. (2015) Banks Are Not Intermediaries of Loanable Funds – and Why This Matters. Working Paper. London: Bank of England.

Labour Party (2015) Manifesto: Britain Can Be Better. At: http://www.labour.org.uk/manifesto.

Lorenz, E. N. (1963) Deterministic Nonperiodic Flow. *Journal of the Atmospheric Sciences*, 20, 130–41.

Lucas, R. E., Jr. (1972) Econometric Testing of the Natural Rate Hypothesis. In: Eckstein, O. (ed.), *The Econometrics of Price Determination Conference, October 30–31, 1970*, Washington, DC: Board of Governors of the Federal Reserve System and Social Science Research Council.

Lucas, R. E., Jr. (1976) Econometric Policy Evaluation:

A Critique. *Carnegie-Rochester Conference Series on Public Policy*, 1, 19–46.

Lucas, R. E., Jr. (2003) Macroeconomic Priorities. *American Economic Review*, 93, 1–14.

McLeay, M., Radia, A. & Thomas, R. (2014) Money Creation in the Modern Economy. *Bank of England Quarterly Bulletin*, Q1, 14–27.

Mian, A. & Sufi, A. (2015) *House of Debt*, Chicago: University of Chicago Press.

Minsky, H. P. (1969) Private Sector Asset Management and the Effectiveness of Monetary Policy: Theory and Practice. *Journal of Finance*, 24, 223–38.

Minsky, H. P. (1972) Financial Instability Revisited: The Economics of Disaster. In: *Reappraisal of the Federal Reserve Discount Mechanism*. Washington, DC: Board of Governors of the Federal Reserve System.

Minsky, H. P. (1977a) A Theory of Systematic Fragility. In: Altman, E. I. and Sametz, A. W. (eds), *Financial Crises*, New York: Wiley-Interscience.

Minsky, H. P. (1977b) The Financial Instability Hypothesis: An Interpretation of Keynes and an Alternative to 'Standard' Theory. *Nebraska Journal of Economics and Business*, 16, 5–16.

Minsky, H. P. (1978) The Financial Instability Hypothesis: A Restatement. *Thames Papers in Political Economy*, Autumn.

Minsky, H. P. (1982) *Can 'It' Happen Again? Essays*

on *Instability and Finance*, Armonk, NY: M.E. Sharpe.

Minsky, H. P. (1986) *Stabilizing an Unstable Economy*, New Haven: Yale University Press.

Nicolis, G. & Prigogine, I. (1971) Fluctuations in Non-equilibrium Systems. *Proceedings of the National Academy of Sciences of the United States of America*, 68, 2102–7.

Obama, B. (2009) Obama's Remarks on the Economy. *New York Times*, 14 April.

O'Brien, Y.-Y. J. C. (2007) Reserve Requirement Systems in OECD Countries. *SSRN eLibrary*.

Ostry, J. D., Loungani, P. & Furceri, D. (2016) Neoliberalism: Oversold? *Finance & Development*, 53, 38–41.

Paulson, H. M. (2010) *On the Brink: Inside the Race to Stop the Collapse of the Global Financial System*, New York: Business Plus.

Pink, B. (2009) Housing Occupancy and Costs. In: STATISTICS, ed. Australian Bureau of Statistics, Canberra.

Prescott, E. C. (1999) Some Observations on the Great Depression. *Federal Reserve Bank of Minneapolis Quarterly Review*, 23, 25–31.

Ramos-Martin, J. (2003) Empiricism in Ecological Economics: A Perspective From Complex Systems Theory. *Ecological Economics*, 46, 387–98.

Romer, P. (2016) The Trouble with Macroeconomics. At:

https://paulromer.net/wp-content/uploads/2016/09/ WP-Trouble.pdf.

Samuelson, P. A. (1956) Social Indifference Curves. *Quarterly Journal of Economics*, 70, 1–22.

Samuelson, P. A. (1966) A Summing Up. *Quarterly Journal of Economics*, 80(4): 568–83.

Sargent, T. J. & Wallace, N. (1976) Rational Expectations and the Theory of Economic Policy. *Journal of Monetary Economics*, 2, 169–83.

Schularick, M. & Taylor, A. M. (2012) Credit Booms Gone Bust: Monetary Policy, Leverage Cycles, and Financial Crises, 1870–2008. *American Economic Review*, 102(2), 1029–61.

Schumpeter, J. (1928) The Instability of Capitalism. *Economic Journal*, 38, 361–86.

Schumpeter, J. A. (1934) *The Theory of Economic Development: An Inquiry Into Profits, Capital, Credit, Interest and the Business Cycle*, Cambridge, MA: Harvard University Press.

Shafer, W. & Sonnenschein, H. (1993) Market Demand and Excess Demand Functions. In: Arrow, K. J. & Intriligator, M. D. (eds), *Handbook of Mathematical Economics*, Amsterdam: Elsevier.

Smets, F. & Wouters, R. (2007) Shocks and Frictions in US Business Cycles: A Bayesian DSGE Approach. *American Economic Review*, 97, 586–606.

Sonnenschein, H. (1972) Market Excess Demand Functions. *Econometrica*, 40, 549–63.

Sraffa, P. (1960) *Production of Commodities by Means of Commodities: Prelude to a Critique of Economic Theory*, Cambridge: Cambridge University Press.

Stevens, G. (2011) The State of Things. *Reserve Bank of Australia Bulletin*, March Quarter, 61–6.

Stock, J. H. & Watson, M. W. (2002) Has the Business Cycle Changed and Why? NBER Working Papers. National Bureau of Economic Research.

Summers, L. (2014) Reflections on the 'New Secular Stagnation Hypothesis'. In: Teulings, C. & Baldwin, R. (eds), *Secular Stagnation: Facts, Causes, and Cures*, London: Centre for Economic Policy Research.

Tremaine, S. (2011) Is the Solar System Stable? At: https://www.ias.edu/about/publications/ias-letter/articles/2011-summer/solar-system-tremaine.

Turner, A. (2016) *Between Debt and the Devil*, Princeton: Princeton University Press.

Vague, R. (2014) *The Next Economic Disaster: Why It's Coming and How to Avoid It*, Philadelphia: University of Pennsylvania Press.

Varian, H. R. (1984) *Microeconomic Analysis*, New York: W. W. Norton.

Varian, H. R. (1992) *Microeconomic Analysis*, New York: W. W. Norton.

Wolf, M. (2014) *The Shifts and the Shocks*, London: Penguin.

Wray, L. R. (2003) Functional Finance and US Government Budget Surpluses in the New Millennium.

# Bibliography

In: Nell, E. J. & Forstater, M. (eds), *Reinventing Functional Finance: Transformational Growth and Full Employment*, Cheltenham and Northampton, MA: Elgar.